T0288399

Oases of Culture

Oases of Culture

A History of Public and Academic Libraries in Nevada

JAMES W. HULSE

UNIVERSITY OF NEVADA PRESS
RENO & LAS VEGAS

Publication of this book was made possible by the
support of the Nevada Library Association.

University of Nevada Press, Reno, Nevada 89557 USA

Copyright © 2003 by University of Nevada Press

Manufactured in the United States of America

Design by Carrie House

Library of Congress Cataloging-in-Publication Data

Hulse, James W.

Oases of culture : a history of public and academic
libraries in Nevada / James W. Hulse.

p. cm.

Includes bibliographical references and index.

ISBN 0-87417-544-5 (alk. paper)

1. Libraries—Nevada—History. 2. Public libraries—
Nevada—History. 3. Academic libraries—Nevada—
History. 4. Nevada State Library and Archives—History.
I. Title.

Z732.N38 H85 2003   027'.009793—dc21

                                    2003000206

The paper used in this book meets the requirements
of American National Standard for Information
Sciences—Permanence of Paper for Printed Library
Materials, ANSI Z39.48-1984. Binding materials were
selected for strength and durability.

FIRST PRINTING

12 11 10 09 08 07 06 05 04 03

5 4 3 2 1

Contents

Illustrations

Preface

The idea of writing a history of Nevada libraries did not originate with me. The inspiration came from Jean Ford, the most energetic nonprofessional friend of libraries in this state in the last quarter of the twentieth century. Her name appears repeatedly in these pages.

Before Ford's work was interrupted by illness in 1997, she called Joan Kerschner, then director of the Nevada Department of Museums, Library, and Arts, to offer a box of files she had gathered as an advocate and self-appointed missionary for public libraries. Ford had inspired the development of libraries in Clark County and elsewhere in Nevada for more than thirty years. Knowing she would not live to use these resources, she asked Kerschner where they should go. Kerschner called me for advice, and I became their custodian. They will be deposited in the state library, in Carson City.

While examining the records, I became acquainted with Helene Cartwright, who had recently arrived in Nevada, attended one of my lectures, and volunteered to help with research as a means of learning more about her adopted state. She became an invaluable assistant in organizing the scattered annals. We soon learned that the Nevada Library Association (NLA), founded in 1946, had assembled thirty-six boxes of material over fifty years,

currently deposited at the University of Nevada, Reno, storage facility at Stead, north of Reno. These records were under the care
of Ellen Guerricagoitia, a library supervisor at UNR who has been
the NLA archivist for many years. The NLA had borrowed space
from the Special Collections division of the UNR Library. I am
grateful to Ms. Guerricagoitia and to Robert Blesse and Susan
Searcy of the UNR Special Collections Department for bringing
the boxes—several at a time—to the main campus, where they
could be indexed by Cartwright. Soon after I began this study, I
found that Martha Gould, former Washoe County librarian, had
scouted the forest earlier and delivered a thoughtful address to her
colleagues in the early 1990s.

Since my first discussions with Ford, I have had productive interviews with hundreds of informants, including Anne Amaral,
Blesse, Bonnie Buckley, Nancy Cummings, Sally Edwards, Carol
and Jack Gardner, Gould, Nancy Hudson, Charles Hunsberger,
Ann Langevin, Clark "Danny" Lee, Alice Lohse, Charles Manley,
Harold Morehouse, Billie Mae Polson, Ellen Reid, and other
members of the guild who have had wide experience in the arena
of library development. I have also had the privilege of meeting
scores of local librarians and assistants willing to share their files
and recollections. These workers manifest a common dedication
to libraries at their best, to the preservation of documents, and to
public service.

The condition of a library is a good indicator of the cultural
maturity of the community it serves. The formation of free public
libraries for general use in the early 1900s was one of the manifes-
tations of the growth of a democratic society. A library can be a
place of self-discovery, entertainment, and empowerment for anyone who walks through its doors or, in these days, visits its databases and resources on the Web.

Special thanks go to several individuals who have made my task
easier. Kerschner repeatedly encouraged me in this effort and tolerated my pesky inquiries. Buckley was generous in sharing the

resources of the State Library and in enabling me to participate in the NLA meeting in Elko in 1999. The kind souls at the Nevada Historical Society in Reno—especially Phil Earl, Eric Moody, and Lee Mortensen—and David Millman at the Nevada State Museum in Las Vegas enabled me to explore data not available elsewhere. I am especially indebted to Manley, of the Washoe County library, who read this manuscript more than once and gave me the benefit of his keen eye. Buckley and Kerschner both gave the manuscript a final reading and made positive suggestions. As usual, my wife, Betty, provided the final, crucial help. Any errors or shortcomings are my own.

My travels around the state allowed me to become acquainted with an admirable array of people from the grass roots (or in Nevada from the sagebrush and mesquite roots) dedicated to the world of books and to the information explosion, of which libraries are a significant component. I have tried to acknowledge many of them later in the text, but I cannot have included all of them. The Nevada guild of librarians, both professional and amateur, is deeply dedicated to serving the rapidly expanding clientele.

Introduction

For the first forty years of the state's existence, most of Nevada was a land devoid of books. For a few lawyers they were rare and costly resources essential to the search for (or evasion of) justice; no public law libraries existed in the earliest days except the one painstakingly assembled at the state capital. The idea that works of literature or technical information might be gathered in a convenient depository at public expense and then lent to readers free of charge with minimum regulations was a concept that did not gain favor until near the end of the nineteenth century. Although the concept was abroad elsewhere, it was not tested in Nevada until 1904, eventually becoming a popular cause in several communities.

At the beginning of the twentieth century, Nevada had a population of forty-two thousand people, about half the number counted a quarter century earlier. By 1900, the state had experienced a severe economic depression for twenty years. Memories of the prosperous 1870s, the era of the Big Bonanza, the fabulous Comstock Lode and the other boom camps were fading.

Just after the turn of the century, however, the zephyrs of social and economic change swept across the state, with the discovery of rich bodies of precious ore at Tonopah and Goldfield and the huge copper beds of White Pine County.[1] Congressman Francis G. Newlands of Reno led the struggle in Congress for the legislation in 1902 that eventually produced the Newlands Reclamation Project and added new agricultural resources to western Nevada's economy. The old political order personified by Comstock-era senators John P. Jones and William M. Stewart, oligarchs of mining and railroad special interests whose careers began during the bonanza years, breathed its last. They had used Nevada as a fiefdom for decades; this ended with their retirements in 1903 and 1905 and made way for the Progressive Era.

During the swan song of the old order, a few Nevada women began to organize in ways unprecedented in the Silver State. Women's social and mutual aid groups arose throughout the state during this era. These efforts blended with the suffrage movement that finally extended the franchise to Nevada women in 1914.[2]

Other populist reforms were also in the making at the turn of the century. The introduction of the referendum, initiative, recall, and primary elections into the law occurred in this era, as did the effort to prohibit gambling and the sale of alcoholic beverages. Several Nevada counties opened high schools for the first time in the early 1900s. Women were at the forefront of many of these movements.

These developments were part of a nationwide transformation that included the emergence of a network of free public libraries. An extensive literature has appeared in the past quarter century that documents and interprets this development. A landmark study, *Apostles of Culture,* written by Dee Garrison and published in 1979, enables us to place the Nevada library developments in a larger context.[3] While Garrison argues that most of the early women leaders within the public libraries between 1876 and 1920 were feminine but not feminists, they laid the foundations of an institution that became one of the seed-beds of social change for women and other socially disfranchised groups in later years. "The genteel library hostess," often a prim and maidenly defender of the male-dominated society, was gradually replaced by the activists of the late twentieth century.

A few favored places in the Far West had the benefit of professionally trained women librarians in the first years of the twentieth century.[4] Nevada's library culture was not developed enough to warrant such learned assistance in those years, but the building of a few tax-supported libraries in Nevada before 1940 was part of a liberating process.

In the same period, the feeble state library went through a metamorphosis, assuming for the first time in the 1890s the functions of a *public* library, as contrasted with a resource restricted to the service of the courts and other government agencies. The creation of taxing authority at the local level for library purposes was part of the populist process; the legislature began hesitantly with a flawed law in 1895, which had to be modified several times before it yielded the desired results in a Reno public library—the first in Nevada—in 1904.

The emergence of the women's suffrage movement paralleled the rise of free public libraries in Nevada and elsewhere; the connection between the two is more than coincidental. "The American Library Association reportedly credited women's clubs with the responsibility for initiating seventy-five per cent of the public libraries in existence in the United States in 1933."[5]

A recent historian of the movement, Lowell A. Martin, a librarian for nearly sixty years, observed that those who established and supported public libraries regarded them as essentially *educational* agencies, "there to help people to understand the world, to prepare them to function as citizens, and to gain information needed for their employment and daily tasks. And education had come to be accepted as public responsibility."[6] The librarian of Congress, James H. Billington, expressed similar sentiments in 1992 when he dedicated the new Nevada State Library and Archives building in Carson City.

Since Nevada was the least populous of states and one of the poorest until the late 1940s, its libraries were among the most primitive in the nation until midcentury. During the following two decades, Nevada's libraries and their custodians, like the parent commonwealth, rose above their chronic malnutrition and grew into healthy community organisms. The purpose of this manuscript is to document and describe that evolution.

The history of libraries should be an integral part of the cultural history of society. The history of Nevada has been greatly enriched in recent decades by the appearance of many new books, monographs, and video studies of the state's unusual cultural milieu. We have seen a surge of new studies on gambling and tourism, on the role of women, on the environment, and a dozen other sub-fields. Jean Ford recognized that the history of libraries, like the bookish institutions themselves, had been neglected in this state, so she collected the raw data in the process of stimulating the public awareness of the importance of libraries and, incidentally, the significance of women in their development.

We will begin our panoramic view in chapter 1 by looking at a few sporadic efforts made by citizens to create private book collections in the frontier mining towns. In the second and third chapters we will examine the history of the Nevada State Library in Carson City, because it provides both an overview and a microcosm of the process of maturation of Nevada's library network. It became, by gradual steps, the caregiver and benefactor of the indigenous, malnourished local libraries across the state.

The fourth chapter will deal with the building of the Washoe County library system. Since Reno pioneered the free library movement and enjoyed the first modest success in Nevada, we will trace its growth over the first ninety-five years.

Chapter 5 offers a perspective on public library development in the fifteen counties once called "rural." The curious biblioholic finds a range of exhibits and experiences of library development here.

The sixth chapter addresses the slow maturation of the libraries in Clark County and the cities within it before 1965 and the dynamic changes of the past thirty years. Finally, we will turn to the libraries of the universities and community colleges.

As of 2001 there were eighty-eight public libraries and eighteen academic libraries listed in the official directory prepared by the Nevada State Library and Archives.[7] This book can deal with only a fraction of them, but it tries for a representative sample. It can only hint at the commitment of the thousands of volunteers and library trustees whose unpaid service has been an essential substructure for every institution under consideration.

The history of Nevada libraries in the twentieth century is a paradigm for the host state. A hundred years ago, Nevada was a desert not only geographically but intellectually.

Billington has written eloquently of the typical community library as "a kind of collective communal tribute to the culture of the book."[8] A century ago such an institution did not exist in Nevada, but as it grew from the native soil that institution was the best oasis for the world's cultural experience on the desert terrain.

Ford's efforts in Clark County in the 1960s reproduced and expanded upon the work of activist women elsewhere before her time on the Nevada frontier and embraced the latest ideas of library science.[9] I hope this synopsis of the evidence is worthy of her efforts and the work of hundreds of others who shared the enterprise in the Silver State. It is offered in gratitude for efforts of generations of under-appreciated librarians who have served aspiring scholars for more than a century.

CHAPTER ONE

The First Forty Years
Pioneering Efforts in Reno and
the Mining Camps

Before public libraries existed, a few mining towns had reading clubs sponsored by fraternal orders or labor unions. In Gold Hill and Virginia City, the Odd Fellows lodges started book collections in 1865 and 1867, respectively. The latter grew to more than two thousand volumes within two years, when the organization decided to make its volumes available to nonmembers who were willing to pay a small fee. The Virginia City lodge also offered periodicals that could be consulted in a quiet smoking room.[1]

The Virginia City Miners' Union, a prominent social organization as well as an industrial advocate, assembled a similar assortment of reading material in the 1870s. Located in a ballroom and games room of the Union Hall on B Street, the collection was started with an allotment of $2,000 in December 1877. Members could use the books without cost; nonmembers could have access by paying fifty cents per month. By 1881 the Miners' Union library had spent $6,000 and owned a collection of twenty-two hundred volumes.[2] This policy reflected the practice common to "subscription libraries" that had been established as early as the eighteenth century in the American colonies.[3] The Miners' Union library was listed as an official depository library of the Department of the Interior as late as 1894.[4]

Literary clubs for purchasing and sharing books emerged in a dozen other mining camps and railroad towns. The instability of these communities and their transient populations made it difficult for literary societies to survive. "One can only guess at the number of 'ghost' libraries left behind when the boom towns faded away," historian Russell R. Elliott wrote.[5]

THE EARLY LAWS

The first law authorizing public libraries to be funded with tax dollars emerged from the Nevada legislature in 1895.[6] The process could be started with a petition, signed by either a majority of the taxpayers or taxpayers who owned more than half of the taxable property within a city, town, or school district. Once a petition was presented to the county commissioners, for example, they were required to impose a small property tax for a library fund. The tax could range from one to five mills on each $100 of assessed valuation and would be administered by a three-man board of library trustees, appointed by the commissioners. Five mills was a minuscule amount of money—not nearly enough to operate even a modest library. The drafter of the final bill undermined the intent of its sponsors by inserting such miserly funding authority.

Yet the 1895 statute was significant because it created the possibility of an independent library board with its own source of tax revenue and with authority to acquire property, erect a building, purchase books, and manage the institution. "Said library and reading room shall forever be and remain free and accessible to the people of such city, unincorporated town or School District, subject to such reasonable rules and regulations as the Library Trustees may adopt," the statute said. The 1895 session also provided, for the first time, for a clerk in the secretary of state's office to act as librarian with a salary of $720 per year.

FRANK NORCROSS

Frank Norcross, one of the three members of the first graduating class of the University of Nevada in 1891 and later a law student at Georgetown University, designed the policy under which public libraries were established for seventy years. He was a supporter of the 1895 law sponsored by Assemblyman S. L. McNaughton of Esmeralda County, which formed the basis of public library policy from 1895 until 1965. He guided that law through several subsequent changes to make it workable.

After his return from law school in Georgetown, Norcross was elected district attorney of Washoe County in 1895–1896. The county owned a parcel of land on the Truckee River at Virginia Street (where the downtown U.S. post office building has stood since the 1930s), which the county commissioners intended to sell but which Norcross struggled to retain as the site for a library. Several years of litigation followed, with Norcross serving as the attorney for those who wanted to hold the property for public use; ultimately he prevailed, in spite of opposition from commissioners.

While serving in the state assembly in 1897, Norcross introduced a bill to amend the defective 1895 statute, significantly increasing the taxing authority of county commissioners for library purposes after a petition had been submitted to them.[7] The bill was easily enacted.

Norcross also assumed the role of fund-raiser. On November 14, 1901, he composed a letter to Andrew Carnegie, the Pittsburgh steel magnate, commenting on Carnegie's previous gifts for public libraries and proposing such a benefaction for Reno.[8] It was a city of between seven thousand and eight thousand people, Norcross said—the largest community between Sacramento and Ogden. It had no library except one at the University of Nevada, which was not open to the public. He provided a cogent argument showing that the community could establish the taxing authority to operate a library if it exercised its right of petition available under state law.

Carnegie's spokesman replied on February 12, 1902, with a question about the population figures Norcross had provided; the census of 1900 reported only forty-five hundred people in Reno. Norcross responded with data about the adjacent Glendale and Brown precincts and statistics from the post office showing a substantial increase in the volume of mail since 1900. Carnegie was satisfied. On March 14 he responded by saying that if the city council would budget $1,500 per year and provide a suitable site, he would furnish $15,000 for the building. By late May, the people of the Reno school district had circulated the petition required by 1897 law, acquired the necessary signatures, and presented them to the court and county commissioners.[9] The $15,000 arrived, and Reno began building its library.

THE CARNEGIE CONCEPT

Carnegie paid for the construction of 1,689 library buildings across the United States, spending more than $41 million (equal to $800 million in 1996).[10] The typical subvention to a community was $10,000, with many larger gifts going to the larger cities.[11] The gift to Reno appears to have been especially generous for a city of its size.

The Carnegie gifts required that the funds be used to build a permanent home for a collection of books available for lending to the public free of charge. The policy also insisted that some form of tax support be provided to guarantee the future operation of the library. Thus the organizers had the assurance that they would not be evicted from temporary or borrowed quarters and that there would be a regular flow of tax money into their coffers. This gave Reno two advantages that many library pioneers in other Nevada communities lacked as they embarked on their book-gathering missions.

When the *Reno Evening Gazette* editorialized about the new building beside the Truckee River that opened in 1904, it assumed that the major function of such an institution was to provide the history, science, and fine literature of the world to those who otherwise would not have such resources available: "History is continually being rewritten as new finds and research put sidelights on the works of yesterday. Science also moves so fast that its tomes are as ephemeral as the hours. Fiction, however, is the most enduring of all and there are read today with kindling interest stories that were penned centuries ago. Yet perhaps scarcely ten books in a century are destined to live."[12]

Norcross subsequently had a fifty-year career in the law that included service as a justice of the Nevada Supreme Court for twelve years and as federal district judge for Nevada for seventeen years.[13] He continued to provide services to Nevada's libraries even as he fulfilled his judicial duties, and he was on hand when the Nevada Library Association was established in 1946.

CHAPTER TWO

The State Library
The First Century, 1865–1965

The Nevada State Library in Carson City, now the nerve center of
the state's public library system, is the oldest repository of books
and official information in the state. Its mission and role have
gradually expanded during its 135-year history. For its first three
decades the so-called library was merely a collection of reference
volumes for the use of officers of the state government. For fifty
years it was an appendage of some other state agency, a legal entity
with little of the substance of its title. For decades after 1895 it tried
to be a full-service lending library to Nevada's scattered population. It has become, by circuitous steps, a vital nucleus of the ma-
ture library system.

The original enumeration of territorial officers in 1861 included an auditor who was also designated as ex officio librarian, a
role that involved few duties during the brief period before Nevada attained statehood in 1864.[1]

The first session of the state legislature in 1865 designated the
secretary of state as ex officio state librarian and made him responsible for the care of "the books, maps, charts, pamphlets and other
documents" owned by the state government. The founding statute
imposed rather rigid rules for the officers who borrowed materials
from the collection. The governor, state controller, and attorney
general constituted a library board to supervise purchases and set

rules.[2] It was conceived only as a support agency for the state officers and courts; its budget was to be derived from fees charged by the secretary of state's office.

This pioneering session, held in 1865 when the population of the state was no more than thirty thousand, also authorized the establishment of "historic, scientific, and literary societies," which did not specifically envision the creation of libraries but assumed their primary mission would be "to promote the diffusion of useful knowledge."[3]

As a branch of the secretary of state's office, the embryonic library began to accumulate records of the state government and such law books as were presumed to be important to the courts. At Virginia City, only fifteen miles from the state capitol, the fabled Big Bonanza of the Comstock Lode appeared and disappeared in the dozen years after the creation of the state and the establishment of its official repository.

Lawmakers searched for decades for a home for the library within the structure of state government. The 1873 legislature assigned the responsibilities of the state library to the lieutenant governor, and the 1875 session appointed the three justices of the Nevada Supreme Court as an ex officio board of directors of the state library, in effect making it an appendage of the judiciary;[4] several later statutes underscored this orientation. A special report on public libraries issued by the Department of the Interior in 1875 indicated that the Nevada State Library held ninety-six hundred volumes.[5]

The 1877 session of the legislature authorized the justices to hire a full-time clerk specifically for the library. Lawmakers of this session seem to have been more studious than their predecessors, as they requested that the library's closing hour be changed from 4 P.M. to 10 P.M. while the legislature was in session.[6]

The collection assembled during the first few years, consisting mainly of law books, was housed in the original capitol, completed in 1871. By 1878 the library needed more space, and it added a room onto the capitol at a cost of $1,300, for which the 1879 leg-islature reimbursed the library fund.

In 1883 the legislature again assigned the lieutenant governor the job of ex officio state librarian. He was made responsible for the expenditure of funds, the management of the books and other materials, and the selection of published material, with a view to what would be most suitable to the wants of the supreme court.[7] The library received many of its books as gifts or in exchanges with other jurisdictions. By the end of the decade the books—especially federal papers—were "in great disorder," as the clerk-librarians struggled to make a catalog for "all the law and miscella-neous books now in this Library."[8]

Lieutenant Governor Joseph Poujade of Pioche, elected in 1890, took a keen interest in the library and wrote a more revealing report than any of his predecessors. Tons of books were being stored in the attic of the capitol, additional space had been developed under the roof, and a single clerk was trying to stay abreast of the increasing workload.[9] For the next two decades much material was stored un-der the dome or in the basement of the capitol.

In 1895, responsibility for the state library was shifted once again to the secretary of state, who by that time was a bookish in-dividual named Eugene Howell. Near the end of his first term in 1898 he wrote:

EXPANDING ITS USE

Since I have taken charge of the Library, I have opened it more generally to the public by extending the privileges of the institution to a larger class of literary people than has been the custom in the past. I considered, that as the respon-sible public are the taxpayers, they should have equal rights with attorneys and others, and I have consequently given the public an opportunity to take advantage of the store of learning that is found on its shelves. The Library is now pa-tronized by twenty persons for every one in the past. I have

on the part of the Library subscribed for all the current literature of the day, in the way of magazines and periodicals. I
have put into the main room a large, polished oak table to be
used only for magazines, so that anyone can come in during
library hours and spend a comfortable hour or two in looking over the articles of the day.[10]

In this otherwise prosaic report is a revolutionary doctrine: that
a library paid for by the citizens for the use of the courts and government bureaus should also be available to citizens for their recreation and information. There is a slightly aristocratic tone to
Howell's report, since he refers to "a larger class of literary people"
and affirms that "the responsible public are the taxpayers," but his
thrust is in the direction of open libraries for the reading public;
even the amateur is entitled to leisure reading at an oak table. This
is a hint at the end of the nineteenth century that the populist
cause had penetrated Nevada, or at least its most refined city.

THE EARLY TWENTIETH CENTURY

Nevada historians often comment on the new vitality and renewed
hope that appeared in Nevada's social and economic life after 1900
as a result of the discovery of ores at Tonopah and Goldfield and in
White Pine County, the development of the federally funded
Newlands Reclamation Project on the Carson and Truckee Riv-
ers, the building of a railroad through southern Nevada, and the
rebuilding of lines through northern Nevada. The cities of Sparks
and Las Vegas were founded in the middle years of this decade. The
population of the state increased from 42,335 in 1900 to 81,875 in
1910.

This was also a transition time for libraries. Two new buildings,
impressive structures for their time, appeared in strategic places.
First, as we have seen, Reno became the home of one of the fa-

mous Carnegie libraries in 1905. In that year the legislature also appropriated money for an octagonal building immediately behind the capitol to accommodate the volumes that had been accumulating in the basement and crowding into the capitol dome. This new structure, intended for the joint use of the library and the supreme court, was dedicated in July 1907. In addition, the first steps were taken in 1905 to found a library in the young town of Tonopah.

Another innovation of 1905 was the enactment of a law that required every county school superintendent to set aside "not less than three dollars nor more than five dollars for each teacher" to be assigned to a district school library fund.[11] At the turn of the century, few schools in the state could claim any kind of library. Orvis Ring, the state superintendent of public instruction, wrote in his biennial report of 1905 that although school trustees had the authority to purchase books for a library, they seldom did so: The trustees "are generally short of funds for the payment of teachers, and cannot think of taking anything out of the treasury for books. Very few schools of this State have anything of a library, some not even a dictionary."[12]

The 1913 report of the state librarian was one of the most exuberant in the annals of that office. The octagonal building was pronounced by Secretary of State George Brodigan to contain "the most complete, 'up-to-date' library west of the Mississippi River and ranking about the sixth best in the United States."[13] This remark, duly noted in some of the leading newspapers, probably reflects the secretary's pride and provincialism more accurately than the quality of the library, but it suggests a substantial improvement in the condition of the collection. The octagon was outfitted with steel bookcases, electric lights, steam heat, and many windows. Both the holdings and the public use of them had increased substantially; the entire collection was said to include fifty thousand volumes. The circulation of the general or "miscellaneous" library (as distinguished from the law library) had grown to more than twenty-six hundred per month. The people of Carson City were obviously making good use of its volumes.

Brodigan tried to keep the "miscellaneous library" abreast of contemporary technology. He reported in 1915 that the youth of Carson City could become proficient as wireless telegraph operators by using the expanded resources. The staff was trying to make scientific and government pamphlets more accessible. The collection had grown to more than 66,546 volumes and 9,823 pamphlets.[14]

PYNE AND HENDERSON, 1915–1930

The 1915 legislature made another change in the management of the library. Removing it from the jurisdiction of the secretary of state, a new law created a State Library Commission, initially composed of the three justices of the Nevada Supreme Court.[15] The director was, for the first time in the state's fifty-year history, an independent administrator working under the supervision of the commission rather than an elected officer assigned the job on an ex officio basis.

The first librarian with this status was Frank J. Pyne, who held the position from 1915 until 1929. One finds in his reports a more professional tone and greater concern for the security of the collection than ever before. The library was financed largely from fees for filings of all official commissions and corporations registered in the secretary of state's office. The 1917 legislature authorized any resident of the state who was vouched for by a taxpayer to borrow books.[16] During this period the library was gradually financed more by direct legislative appropriation and less by fines and fees.

Pyne's successor was V. M. Henderson (1929–1935), whose reports are less hopeful and less informative than those of Pyne during the 1920s. Once again the collection was outgrowing the space available in the octagonal building, and makeshift arrangements were required to store the books. The impact of the Great Depression tempered the hopes of the custodian for a collection still perceived to be one of the best in the West.[17]

By the early 1930s the octagonal building was obviously inadequate, and when federal funds in the amount of about $37,000 became available, the 1935 legislature authorized construction of a new building for the supreme court and library on the west side of Carson Street directly opposite the capitol. The white art deco structure was in sharp contrast to the sandstone of the capitol and the other government buildings on Carson Street. It had formidable metal doors bearing the Great Seal of Nevada and black marble encasing the entryway. It was an architectural affirmation that Nevada was evolving beyond its pioneering days.

E. CHARLES D. MARRIAGE, 1935–1950

Before the move into the new building was complete, commissioners appointed the third librarian, E. Charles D. Marriage, formerly the publisher of a newspaper in Caliente. Although not a professional librarian, he was a man with a vision, a taste for good literature, and sense of history.[18]

Marriage had an instinct for a policy that later generations would call "outreach." Like Howell forty years earlier, he was keen to serve the remote public as well as the official community in Carson City. Beginning in 1938 and for several years thereafter, the biennial report of the State Library Commission listed the local libraries established by the counties and cities and provided numbers indicating the size of their collections. At that time Nevada had seven county and three city libraries in operation, and one county branch library at Sparks.

Marriage prepared this list on the local libraries in 1940:[19]

LIBRARIES	LOCATION	NO. OF BOOKS
County		
Churchill	Fallon	5,000
Elko	Elko	8,000
Humboldt	Winnemucca	3,500
Lyon	Yerington	13,000
Washoe	Reno	70,365[20]
White Pine	Ely	10,000
Lincoln	Pioche	1,500
City		
Tonopah	Tonopah	3,753
Las Vegas	Las Vegas	14,500
Boulder City	Boulder City	6,524
Sparks (A branch of Washoe County)		
University of Nevada		
Clark Memorial Library	Reno	63,210
Mackay School of Mines	Reno	14,300
Agricultural Division	Reno	5,000
State		
Nevada State Library	Carson City	236,527

There was one hint of the future in this same report. The state library had received a gift of $3,000 from Major Max C. Fleischmann of Glenbrook in 1938 to assist the rural libraries. This evidence of Fleischmann's interest in libraries was a portent.

In the mid-1930s, the state library received assistance from the federal government for staff personnel. As state budgets had been chronically inadequate to allow the staff to process the growing collection, the federal help was a major boost. Another innovation of the late 1930s was use of New Deal programs to make more opportunities available for young people frustrated by the Great

Depression. In 1940 Marriage reported that branch libraries funded by the National Youth Administration were operating in Alamo, Austin, Baker, Battle Mountain, Desert Silver, Eureka, Fernley, Genoa, Gerlach, Imlay, Lake Tahoe (Zephyr Cove), Lovelock, Montello, Panaca, Rio Tinto, and Virginia City. This program was suspended in 1942 because of the outbreak of World War II.

Demands on the state library increased from all directions during the war. In 1942, without the fiscal resources to process the new materials, it became a depository for all documents issued by the federal superintendent of documents.

In 1946, when the state's population stood at about 130,000, Marriage reported that the list of registered borrowers stood at 19,132, "residing, for the most part, in the smaller communities of Nevada. There are 124 post offices in the State and library records show that requests for books were received from every office. To properly serve these patrons the State Library should institute bookmobile service; a bill for this purpose was introduced in the 1945 Legislature and died in committee."[21]

Marriage became a diligent promoter of libraries, seeking to persuade the governor and legislature to embrace a broader vision of service to the reading public. He was one of the leading co-founders of the Nevada Library Association in 1946, and he developed an active program of trying to assist schools. He died in 1950. During his productive, fifteen-year tenure the library took seriously its duties as a statewide service institution.

THE NEVADA LIBRARY ASSOCIATION

Efforts to build a more effective network of libraries after World War II drew crucial energy from the corps of workers within the Nevada Library Association. Established under the leadership of six librarians from the Reno–Carson City area,[22] the NLA became the grass roots organization that complemented the efforts of the state library and enabled the professionals in larger communities to work more effectively with their struggling, isolated counterparts around the state. It evolved into a network for sharing information from other parts of the country, a lobbying force in Carson City and Washington, and a forum for camaraderie among professionals and volunteers scattered across the state. Previously the library pioneers had been like individual trekkers across the desert wasteland, with an occasional helping hand from the state. When they organized, the librarians and their boards learned and demonstrated the value of a caravan.

The small cluster of devotees who assembled for the first meeting in Reno on June 4–5, 1946, regarded themselves as trailblazers because Nevada was the last state in the Union to form such an association. In attendance was retired Federal Judge Frank Norcross, promoter of the free library legislation of the 1890s and father of the Reno Carnegie library in 1904–1905. Governor Vail Pittman was also present as a testimonial of his tacit support, but the state government was still many years away from providing tangible policies and funding to aid libraries beyond the work the state library had traditionally done.

Edwin Castagna, the Washoe County librarian, became the first president and state librarian; Marriage the president-elect. James Hill, director of the university library, was named secretary-treasurer. Representatives from several outlying counties comprised the board of directors.[23]

Among its first actions, the NLA announced its support for a bill pending in Congress for a "library demonstration program" to assist states in improving their services, especially in rural areas, with modest sums for library development. They discussed plans for book exchanges, for an improved state library law, and for workshops at the university to train individuals for service.

Castagna was an energetic president. He studied the laws of other states for examples that might be applied in Nevada, and he toured rural Nevada to learn about the situations in the local libraries. He found most of them to be mere "repositories for ragged books."[24] The main sources of support were in the Parent-Teachers' Associations, the Association of University Women, and the Federation of Women's Clubs.

In 1949, the legislature enacted a law abolishing the library commission and requiring that any future state librarian have professional experience and library school training.[25]

THE NATIONAL SCENE AT MID-CENTURY

At the national level, the American Library Association (ALA) had become a champion of the First Amendment rights for librarians and their patrons. Having adopted a Library Bill of Rights in 1939, it set a standard for librarians that encouraged them to become vigorous opponents of censorship. One of the best historical descriptions of this process was written by Castagna, who had followed his tenure in the Reno library with a career in the East, including a term as head of the ALA.[26]

The ALA also inspired an institutional self-examination at the end of the 1940s, issuing a report on the status of public libraries in the United States. The study was endorsed by the Social Science Research Council and financed by the Carnegie Foundation. Directed by Robert D. Leigh, a political scientist, it was called the Public Library Inquiry.[27] It provided much technical data and advice; in addition, at times it became visionary and lyrical. Libraries were involved in more than entertainment and education, the report affirmed; they were also becoming important as instruments of communication, taking their place along with newspapers, magazines, pamphlets and documents, recordings, radio, motion pictures, and television.[28] The study conceived of an interlocking web of public, school, and research libraries that would serve each other and their clients through a single cooperative system. Leigh could not have anticipated the Internet, but his vision embraced the concept: "The three networks of library service, public, school and research, when fully developed, would provide people of all ages in all places with abundant opportunity to learn so far as library materials can give that opportunity."[29]

It was a dream fifty years ahead of its time. Meanwhile Nevada, still at a primitive stage in library development in 1950, began to engage in its own introspection.

NEVADA LIBRARIANS LOOK IN THE MIRROR: THE 1950S

Constance C. Collins succeeded Marriage as state librarian. She was the first occupant of that office to hold a professional library science degree and the first woman named to the job.[30] Collins personified a rising breed of trained feminine librarians who brought higher stature to a service that had been chronically undervalued.[31]

She accelerated the policies of outreach not only within Nevada but also with the federal government and other states. Her reports reflect the values of a specialist, concerned about improving the catalog, maintaining the collection, and improving the quality of assistance to the public. A recurring theme of her reports was "service to all Nevadans."

Twice during the 1950s the state government took a close, critical look at its library policies and resources. In each case the studies focused on shortcomings that had long been evident to those dedicated to public service in the realm of books.

In 1953 Assemblywoman Hazel B. Denton of Caliente sponsored a resolution asking the Legislative Counsel Bureau to make a survey of the condition of Nevada libraries and the state laws affecting them.[32] The result was an extensive internal review not only of libraries but also of cultural resources. This study had the participation of the administrators of a dozen agencies concerned with the schools, the university, the museums and historical society, as well as the libraries.[33] The judgment was that the public libraries were very feeble as places of learning and enlightenment and that the means for distributing the available books were inadequate.

Another significant conclusion was that existing state law discouraged local autonomy in library development and related matters; it inhibited rather than encouraged initiative because of the requirements that a majority of taxpayers or taxpayers representing a majority of the taxable property must sign a petition to mandate a local tax for libraries.[34] The 1895 law as amended, originally seen as a means of demonstrating public support for libraries, now constituted a de facto veto power that out-of-state property owners might exercise against a local population taking such initiative. The legislative counsel team concluded that Nevada had no adequate policy or resources for the preservation of archives and no means of coordinating the work of museums and historical groups whose functions complemented the libraries. The recommendation was not fully implemented until the 1990s, when the legislature enacted laws creating a Department of Museums, Library, and Arts.

State librarian Collins was a leading participant in the work of this 1954 study and also had an important role in the next survey, made five years later. In 1958, she contracted with an out-of-state professional consultant for an analysis of all the public libraries in the state and for recommendations about how to improve the small but growing network. The consultant, Gretchen Knief Schenk of Summerdale, Alabama, prepared an overview unprecedented in its scope and detail.[35] Her sixty-two-page benchmark document provided guidance for developing a coordinated statewide program for several years.

Since Nevada's population exceeded 250,000 by the late 1950s, it was evident that the reading resources available to the public were not keeping pace with the growth. The survey revealed great variations in the kind and quality of library service available across

the state. Eleven Nevada counties had some form of freely circulating book collection supported by local taxes in 1958, although
in some cases the budgets for book purchases were meager or
nonexistent. Esmeralda, Eureka, Lander, Storey, Douglas and
Ormsby Counties had no local libraries.[36] (The latter three, however, were near the state library, and resident book lovers had access
to that venerable institution.)

Schenk found distressing conditions in most libraries. Widely
differing policies existed on budgets and book selections; many
had a heavy emphasis on "the popular best-seller type of literature"
and a paucity of periodicals, dictionaries, encyclopedias, and other
reference material. Most collections were located in overcrowded
or inconvenient housing. Only six professional librarians were
employed in the entire state. "Bookmobiles," Schenk wrote, "have
so far been an unknown quantity in Nevada."[37]

The results of her survey convinced Schenk that the state library could no longer be expected to serve the entire state as it had
traditionally tried to do. It was trying to be "the reservoir of books
and other materials from which other libraries of the state can
draw."[38] The burden and expectations placed on its small staff were
heavy, but great strides had been made during the 1950s because
the staff had been increased from three to eight. Once again the
"new" library quarters built in 1935 were overcrowded.

One of the few positive factors Schenk emphasized was the
dedication of the small cadre of librarians and library board members to the cause of building better facilities and providing better
service to the public.

After giving this candid and discouraging description of the existing resources, Schenk offered positive suggestions. A more ratio-
nal and equitable funding system was needed, she concluded; she
proposed a property tax of 10 cents per $100 of assessed valuation
throughout the state. The existing law provided for a rate of no less
than 5 cents but no more than 15, but there was no minimum for
maintenance. Nevada should find the means and the will to train

more professional librarians, she said, sending some of its own to other states if necessary; a voluntary system of certification was needed.

The report proposed a regional service plan to combine the resources and promote cooperation among scattered institutions in the northeastern, the west-central, and the southern parts of the state, with service centers in Elko, Reno, and Las Vegas.[39] A division of this kind was adopted a few years later with only slight modifications of Schenk's recommendations.

She made specific suggestions for improvements in the library laws and for a centralized procedure for processing new books, with the state library offering standardized service to local libraries.[40] State librarian Joseph F. Schubert initiated this latter recommendation in 1959.

The candid analyses of the 1950s yielded timely results. Some bills passed by the 1959 session of the legislature bear the imprint of Schenk's recommendations. The new laws authorized intercounty cooperation, a 10-cent tax rate, and clarifications of the authority of local library boards.[41]

In addition, Congress had passed the Library Services Act (LSA) in 1956, which authorized federal funds to help local governments build and expand library facilities in rural areas. This was of limited value to Nevada in the short run but became more important in the following decade. One of the primary sponsors of this legislation was Congressman Cliff Young, who made an eloquent statement about the needs of Nevada libraries.[42] Nevada presented its plan for the use of federal funds almost immediately after President Dwight D. Eisenhower signed the bill into law, but the modest appropriation and the failure of the state to provide matching funds was disappointing.

If the 1950s were years of self-assessment, healthy criticism, and planning for the Nevada library community, the 1960s were a time of dramatic advancement in building a cooperative network, with the state library as the catalyst.

CHAPTER THREE

Since 1965
The State Library, the Nevada Library Association, and Fleischmann Gifts

Libraries are organic creatures; they outgrow their garments all too soon. One might surmise that a thirty-year cycle was operating for Nevada libraries during the first one hundred years of statehood. The facilities for most book collections in the modest rooms initially provided became inadequate after about three decades. The responsible custodians were sorely challenged to meet their obligations to clients and the materials on their shelves. Money for library construction always lagged behind the obvious needs of the expanding reading public.

In 1965, the Nevada Council on Libraries commissioned a study on the condition of libraries in the state, which provides an interesting comparison with the data compiled by state librarian Marriage twenty-five years earlier. The 1965 profile found that, even though the library network had grown, the number of books per capita statewide had declined in the previous few years because the population was expanding much more rapidly than the libraries were.[1]

Nevada's population more than tripled between 1940 and 1965, from about 110,000 to approximately 380,000. The number of its public libraries grew from eleven to twenty. Potential patrons in the suburbs of Las Vegas and in distant rural places were served poorly, if at all. Citizens of the unincorporated areas of Clark

County (with about 80,000 people) were still without a publicly supported library in the early 1960s, unless they made special arrangements with someone on the city library staff. Most towns outside the county seats in the rural counties were likewise without a local oasis of books and lending service, having to wait for a bookmobile to come their way occasionally.

As the population of the state grew from 285,000 to 488,000 between 1960 and 1970, those who worked within cultural and educational institutions struggled to accommodate the surge of new residents. Fortunately the Max C. Fleischmann Foundation of Nevada appeared with its series of major gifts to local libraries, providing millions for new buildings or improvements in a dozen communities.

In addition to this windfall, significant support became available to local governments after 1964 from federal sources under the Library Services and Construction Act (LSCA), an expansion and liberalization of the 1956 act (LSA). This law was part of President Lyndon B. Johnson's Great Society program. More flexible than its predecessor, the LSCA brought larger amounts of federal construction money for local libraries. Meanwhile the state library became more proficient and more professional in the help it could offer to public libraries.

It is a basic fact of life that the crucial support for libraries came from outside—from private gifts or federal funding—rather than from the tax resources of Nevada.

THE STATE LIBRARY AFTER 1965

The law books and the "miscellaneous" (i.e., literary, scientific, and popular) collection in Carson City continued to grow despite budget constraints. In the early 1960s, the state library was once again cramped in the space that had been provided twenty-five years earlier. Schubert, the state librarian from 1959 to 1961 who then took a position with the ALA in Chicago, served for too short a time to address this problem. He did, however, initiate a cooperative system among northern Nevada libraries known as the Silver Circle, a precursor of the later innovations that put this state ahead of most others in integrated services.

Schubert's successor in 1962 was Mildred J. Heyer, a former Las Vegas schoolteacher and an able leader whose energy and initiative were challenged by myriad expanding requirements for research and advisory services from the courts and state agencies. As the state's population approached 400,000 in the mid-1960s, both the supreme court and library urgently needed more room.

Some library departments were shifted to temporary quarters elsewhere in Carson City. Heyer decided the library, which had gradually scaled back its lending services to distant patrons, could no longer provide local lending service for citizens of Ormsby and Douglas Counties, and this practice ended in 1966. The acquisitions department stopped buying fiction, popular nonfiction, and juvenile works, leaving those categories to the local levels.[2] It did, however, expand its concentration on interlibrary loan services and research and advisory work for government agencies and local public libraries.

Heyer placed greater emphasis on helping the county and city libraries become more self-sufficient in reference resources and less dependent on Carson City. She promoted workshops and training sessions through the Nevada Library Association and a program of voluntary certification.

THE RESTRUCTURING OF 1965

The 1965 session of the legislature—its centennial—was the most important in the history of the state in removing the legal shackles that restricted the development of public libraries. Leaders of the NLA recognized that local library improvement was retarded because local governments lacked the authority to borrow money for construction without a special act of the legislature. As regular sessions were held only every two years for nine or ten weeks, a small opportunity existed for the counties and cities to get their plans in order and make their case to the lawmakers.

In December 1964, three library activists in Reno drafted a proposal for the NLA advocating a new law in 1965 to authorize counties to issue bonds for library construction without a special act of the legislature. Bill Andrews, Washoe County librarian, Alice Lohse, and Portia Griswold wrote a proposal for the NLA recommending annual appropriations for library development in addition to the meager amounts typically provided for operations. "Almost no Nevada county has adequate quarters to provide free, public library service to its residents," their report said.[3] The NLA—then in its twentieth year—had matured considerably. NLA members were learning to retrain themselves, to improve their skills as the new technologies demanded, to remain sensitive to the needs of the changing community, and to sharpen their political savvy.

They also asked for the creation of a Nevada Council on Libraries consisting of the state librarian and six members of the NLA appointed by the governor. The proposal was written into the law in 1965, authorizing the council to meet twice a year to prepare an overview on the state of libraries, on statistics, resources, and education possibilities for librarians, and on related matters.[4] The state library was designated as secretariat of the council, which was responsible to the governor and invited to make recommendations to the legislature for measures to enhance library service. The NLA had a role in the nominating process and became a partner in gathering information and suggesting policy.[5] The council had broad authority to receive gifts on behalf of libraries.

The 1965 legislature broke new ground in two other areas. It liberalized the laws fashioned by Norcross between 1895 and 1901 to enable Reno to begin its public library, making it much easier to establish special library districts by petition. This move was initiated by library advocates from Clark County. (We will deal with this innovation in chapter 6.)

This session also permitted the establishment of regional library systems,[6] an idea that had been proposed by Schenk in 1958. This allowed for joint administration of the libraries in Elko, Eureka, and Lander Counties.

THE FLEISCHMANN FOUNDATION

The greatest boon to Nevada libraries from 1965 through 1980 was the Max C. Fleischmann Foundation of Nevada. Fleischmann was a businessman who had made a fortune in the food and beverage industry and established a well-endowed trust before his death in 1951. Because Nevada offered a tax shelter for millionaires, he chose Glenbrook at Lake Tahoe as his place of legal residence during the last years of his life. He took a keen interest in cultural, educational, conservation, and humanitarian affairs and had a special fondness for Nevada's fishing holes, terrain, and culture. He selected as trustees for his legacy a few individuals whom he respected and who shared his priorities. They granted more than $8 million to local governments in Nevada to build or assist eighteen libraries.

The trustees of the foundation began their major gifts to libraries in the early 1960s with a $1,392,804 grant for the new Washoe County library building on South Center Street. A few years later they made a similar contribution to the newly created Clark County Library District, enabling it to build its first permanent home on East Flamingo Boulevard. Gifts to the Ormsby County (Carson City) library in 1969 and 1980 totalled $1.1 million, and the Douglas County libraries received $1,066,823. In rural Nevada, the Fleischmann grants for local library construction approached $4 million.[7] A dozen towns were thus able to plan and build spacious new, well-lighted local edifices for books, some with cathedral-like ceilings affording a sharp contrast to the typical dark, cramped quarters that most Nevada librarians and their patrons

had known in the past. (Some of these gifts to individual communities will be discussed in chapter 5.) The gifts to the University of
Nevada in Reno included a building for the College of Agriculture, with space for a life sciences library to serve the biological
sciences and nursing as well as traditional agriculture.

In addition to its grants for buildings, the foundation contributed generously to the long-range planning process initiated in
the 1960s for the purchase of historical materials for a university
book-fund drive and for community college learning resource
centers. It also bought bookmobiles for outlying areas where library service was not easily accessible.

THE 1970S AT THE STATE LIBRARY

Joe Anderson was state librarian through most of the 1970s, the
most challenging period in the institution's history. Late in 1972 it
was forced to relocate from the art deco building that had been its
home for thirty-seven years into the old federal courthouse a few
blocks north on the opposite side of Carson Street. Librarians lost
control of the moving process when state workers, assigned the
task of transferring the collection, crammed volumes and papers in
boxes pell mell and stored them in a jumble in warehouses while
the next quarters were being made ready.

The old courthouse, built in the 1890s, proved to be even less
satisfactory than the former site. Charming though it was with its
red brick façade looming over the neighborhood, its floors had
not been designed to hold tons of books. Librarians wore hard hats
for months to reduce the risk of injury from falling plaster. Much
of the responsibility for putting the collection in order fell to Joan
Kerschner and Martha Gould, two newcomers who became influ-
ential figures on the Nevada library scene for the next twenty-five
years.

The staff managed to reopen the library in the summer of 1973 after retrieving scattered books and documents from snowed-in trailers and insecure warehouses, where they had been hastily stored. Although its quarters were inadequate, the library staff was poised—none too soon—for the onset of the computer revolution.

During the decade of the 1970s, the age of automation entered the quiet domain of libraries as into all other aspects of advanced society, and the time-tested methods of purchasing, cataloging, and lending were revolutionized. Libraries became high-tech operations. Pioneers in the field of automation included Charles Hunsberger of the Clark County Library District, Robert Anderl of the UNLV library, Joyce Ball of the UNR library, Gould of the Washoe County library, and Kerschner of the state library. They were among the first "techies"—the light-hearted label applied to those who began to adapt the evolving computer technology to Nevada libraries. In 1979 the public services department of the state library funded a study to prepare for the transition to electronic catalogs. Within the next few years Nevada developed a statewide telecommunications system linking all public and academic data bases, with Kerschner and Gould as the key planners. Nevada was in the vanguard among the fifty states in linking its public libraries with cooperative purchasing and lending through the emerging technology.

The league of librarians that matured in Nevada had another opportunity to take a close look at themselves and their services late in 1978 at a governor's conference on library and information needs. Governor Mike O'Callaghan assembled the gathering to stimulate better community input in library development. One hundred delegates, two-thirds of them non-librarians, assembled in Las Vegas. This was a prelude to a White House conference on libraries.

The pressures for a library network more worthy of a booming state mounted during the early 1980s, but the guild faced several dark hours before the public gave them a rousing mandate. The library community supported an effort to pass a major bond issue in

1982, but the measure failed by a narrow vote. Emissaries from the NLA got a mixed reception when they went before the 1983 legislature, seeking a more adequate tax base. Legislators did allow a $10 million library construction bond proposal to be placed before the voters in 1984. This new measure went on the ballot (Question Nine) with the expectation that it had a modest chance for success.

THE 1984 SURPRISE

This time library advocates prepared their case more effectively, and the public approved the bond issue overwhelmingly. The vote was 152,245 in favor and 114,572 opposed—a meaningful victory, because in the same election voters rejected two other financial proposals that would have involved public expenditures. The fact that the Fleischmann Foundation had built high-quality facilities in so many communities and was then concluding its work was probably a factor in the high level of support.

The distribution of bond money became controversial because of competition among local libraries for the largess. The Nevada Council on Libraries recommended the distribution of the money based upon a formula set by law. The statute required local money equal to the state funds.[8] As Las Vegas and Clark County had a tax structure that provided a dependable source of income for matching money, their libraries received $7.15 million for capital improvements. The Henderson Library District received $1.93 million; Elko County library got $360,000; Washoe County library, $99,000; and $450,000 was reserved for grants to rural counties.[9] The basic fact was that Clark County had built a much stronger financial base for its libraries than Washoe County had, because a $15 million bond issue had recently been approved in the southern county.

The pill was especially difficult for Washoe library boosters to swallow because that county had voted more decisively in favor of the library bonds than had any other county in the state; in fact, a majority of voters in all counties except Washoe and Clark opposed the bond issue.

Newspaper columnist Guy Shipler, one of the most astute members of the Nevada journalism fraternity, wrote that the strong showing of support for Question Nine made the legislators of 1985 much more attentive to the need of libraries.[10] Library advocates had smoother sailing than usual in the next few sessions of the legislature.

THE KERSCHNER ERA

Kerschner was a key figure in the evolution of Nevada libraries throughout the 1980s and 1990s. Having begun her Nevada career as a teacher and librarian in Las Vegas, she joined the state library staff as documents librarian in 1973. Gradually assuming added responsibility for public services and administrative work, she rose through the ranks steadily. Her knowledge of the various state agencies and her political skills made her the obvious candidate for the top position when Anderson died. Governor Richard Bryan appointed her state librarian in 1986.

Seven years later, when the legislature consolidated the library with the historical organizations and museums,[11] Governor Bob Miller designated her as director of the Department of Museums, Library, and Arts even as she continued as state librarian. She held this dual appointment until 1999, when she resigned to become the director of the Henderson Library District.

The most tangible achievement during her tenure was the building of the expansive new library and archives edifice on Stewart Street on the east side of the capitol complex. When the old federal courthouse became the "temporary" home of the library in 1973, the staff believed their forced sojourn there would last no more than ten years; instead they were forced to endure their cramped quarters twice that long. By the 1980s the functions of the library were scattered among four different buildings, all inadequate.

The legislature finally addressed the needs in 1987 when it appropriated $790,000 to plan a 136,000-square-foot building. The architectural firm of DeLorenzo, Sticha and Associates designed the new facility. Ground was broken in February 1990, and the new edifice—a modern steel-and-glass structure that offered compensation for the decades of overcrowded quarters suffered by the staff and collection—opened for public access in January 1993. Its spacious, soaring foyer with a striking view onto the capitol grounds could hardly have been more unlike the rabbit warren conditions in which librarians had toiled for two decades. Symbolically, it was constructed around the old State Archives building, which became the repository of the Nevada Constitution of 1864.

At the cornerstone ceremony held on October 31 (Nevada Day), 1992, the keynote speaker was James H. Billington, librarian of Congress and a noted historian. Summarizing the challenges of the new age and the place of libraries within it, he emphasized the links between past and future and among peoples of a variegated culture:

> Economic growth in this country is largely recorded in information-based enterprise. That uniquely American institution, the open public library has a central role to play in this coming Age of Information. This world of information is bewildering, sometimes overwhelming. It is essentially now a rapidly growing network of increasingly available raw material for the inquiring mind. . . .

> To be true to ourselves, we Americans must preserve the values of the old book culture even as we reap the benefit of the new electronic networking. Humanism and democracy, if they are to be sustainable on a continental scale and in a multicultural context, must have some *shared* common values and, at the same time, real tolerance for variety and difference.

And that is precisely what the open American library repre-
sents.[12]

In the first ten years of Kerschner's administration, approximately $120 million was spent in Nevada for the construction of
new facilities in various parts of the state.

Many of the urban and rural libraries that opened or expanded
or computerized during this period relied on the state library for
advice and for the administration of state and federal grant money.
Kerschner, in the tradition of most of her predecessors, took a
keen interest in the needs of the scattered rural libraries. She trav-
eled as often as possible to outlying counties and cities and coop-
erated with the local staffs in obtaining federal funds and organizing their collections. She was much more fortunate than her
predecessors because the state legislature took greater interest in library matters.

When Kerschner resigned in 1999 to become director of the
Henderson district libraries, she was replaced by Monteria
Hightower, previously a regional administrator in the Las Vegas–
Clark County Library District. Hightower had been a primary
proponent, as chair of the government relations committee of NLA,
of a statewide policy enacted by the 1997 legislature that enabled
local libraries to apply to the state library for support funding for
the purchase of books, library materials, and databases. A total of
$2.4 million was appropriated from the general fund for this
project, half to be awarded in each of the 1998 and 1999 fiscal
years.

THE ELECTRONIC ERA

In the early 1980s, the preliminary steps that Nevada had taken in
the automation and computerization of its library collections began to bear fruit. The state library provided leadership for the development of the Cooperative Libraries Automated Network

(CLAN). The network began as an arrangement for sharing computer resources between the state library and the Carson City and Churchill County libraries and evolved into a consortium of fifteen northern Nevada institutions that shared computer systems and databases with one another. CLAN has made it possible for the libraries to have a single online catalog for information retrieval, cooperative circulation and cataloging activity, and shared licensing of commercial databases, enabling these institutions to reduce many of the basic costs of processing their materials.

The state library publishes an annual directory of Nevada libraries and pertinent statistics, regular masterplans for suggested development, and brochures for the state data center, and manages programs to improve literacy throughout the state.

THE NEVADA LIBRARY ASSOCIATION

Since its founding in 1946, the NLA has matured as an effective advocate not only for better funding and more progressive laws for local libraries but also a voice against censorship and a vehicle to spread the benefits of reading and literacy within the larger community. Incorporated by the legislature in 1963,[13] it has worked in partnership with the state library in serving the scattered tax-supported book repositories across the state. NLA leaders have been active participants in every major study done on library needs in the past half century.[14]

The NLA divides its work into four areas that focus on the concerns of: 1) academic and specialized research libraries, 2) public libraries, 3) library trustees, and 4) children's services. In addition, the association is the vehicle that enables individual libraries to remain in touch through a regular newsletter and annual meetings. Its conventions are normally held in the autumn in different regions, and hundreds of members participate.

One of the least appreciated services provided by the NLA is its work as a guardian of the peoples' right to read material of their choice. Since at least 1962 the NLA has devoted much of its energy and talent to the ongoing struggle for the liberty to make available materials of a controversial nature. In that year the association formed a Committee for Intellectual Freedom. Frequently, self-appointed guardians of the public morals object to some of the reading matter on library shelves. All too often legislation is considered that proposes censorship by or for librarians, and the NLA has been in the vanguard of those opposing such restrictions. In 1981 the NLA persuaded the legislature to enact a law to protect the confidentiality of library users. Following the guidelines of the *American Library Association's Library Bill of Rights,* the NLA has developed its own *Intellectual Freedom Handbook,* issued in 1984 and 1994 under the leadership of Lynn Ossolinski and expanded again in 1999 as a guide for libraries and their staffs. It insists upon the right to privacy for library users and resists all efforts by meddlers to learn about the materials individuals are reading. In 1999 the NLA under the leadership of Bonnie Buckley took another stand for freedom of access to Internet materials.

STATE ARCHIVES

The Division of State Archives, established under the secretary of state's jurisdiction in 1965 as a repository for official documents of historical importance, had a shaky existence from the start. Not adequately funded in the early years and lacking the kind of professional care that archival work requires, this collection was transferred to the control of the state library in 1979. About two years later the Nevada State Library formally became Nevada State Library and Archives. In 1980, Guy Louis Rocha, who had recently earned a master of arts in history from UNR, was appointed archivist. Rocha approached his challenge vigorously, rescuing long-neglected documents from unsafe surroundings and developing professional systems for preservation, retrieval, and research service of neglected documents. For the first time Nevada had a records management program and a policy for retention and disposal of official records. The opening of the Nevada State Library and Archives building on Stewart Street in 1993 gave this division state-of-the-art facilities. Rocha proved to be a prolific writer on Nevadiana, a debunker of myths, and a skillful radio interviewer, in addition to performing his duties as archivist.

The state archives division receives, for example, all the records of the governor's office as soon as a change of administration occurs. The range of archival responsibilities is broad; the archives holds the papers of scores of cities and counties, defunct and active state agencies, as well as those of the nuclear waste dump near Beatty. It has the responsibility for preserving some of these records for many centuries in the future.

Public Libraries in Nevada, 2000. Map by Kris Pizarro, based on *Nevada Library Directory and Statistics: 2000.* Courtesy Kris Pizarro.

Four sites of the Nevada State Library in Carson City: 1) In the capitol (c. 1871–1913);
2) in the octagonal building behind the capitol (c. 1913–1935); 3) in the art deco building
across the street from the capitol (1936–1972); and 4) in the facility on Stewart Street fore-
ground. (1992–). From 1972 to 1992, the library was located in the old federal court
building on Carson Street. Courtesy Nevada State Library and Archives.

Frank Norcross about
1910, founder of Reno
Public Library. From Sam
P. Davis, ed., *The History
of Nevada* (Reno: Elms
Publishing Co., 1913).

(*top left*) Joan Kerschner, state librarian 1986–1999. Courtesy Joan Kerschner.

(*top right*) Jean Ford. Courtesy Nevada Women's Fund.

(*right*) E. Charles D. Marriage, state librarian 1935–1950. From James G. Scrugham, *Nevada: A Narrative of the Conquest of a Frontier Land* (Chicago: American Historical Society, 1935).

Reno Carnegie Library, c. 1905. Courtesy Nevada Historical Society.

First Las Vegas courthouse, which housed the city library 1916–1951. Courtesy Squires Collection, James Dickinson Library, UNLV.

First Henderson library, c. 1946. Courtesy James Dickinson Library, UNLV.

The Henderson library, dedicated 2002. Courtesy Henderson District Public Library.

The Fleischmann library in Minden. Courtesy Douglas County Library.

The Fleischmann library in Fallon. Courtesy Churchill County Library.

Interior of Reno downtown library, c. 1968. Courtesy Hwa-Di Brodhead.

Rainbow branch, Las Vegas–Clark County Library District. Courtesy Las Vegas–Clark County Library District.

Lied Library, University of Nevada, Las Vegas. Courtesy UNLV Photo Service.

(*opposite page, top*) First Clark County library. Courtesy Las Vegas–Clark County Library District.

(*opposite page, bottom*) Main Library, University of Nevada, Reno, 1987. Courtesy Special Collections, Getchell Library, University of Nevada, Reno.

The founding of a library is one of the greatest things we can do...

Everyone able to read a good book becomes a wiser man...

A collection of good books contains all the nobleness & wisdom of the world before us. A collection of books is the best of all universities.... Thomas Carlyle

Great Basin College Library, Elko. Courtesy Great Basin College Library.

(*opposite page, top*) Miner's Union Hall, Virginia City, site of Nevada's first private subscription library. Courtesy Nevada Historical Society.

(*opposite page, bottom*) The opening of the Las Vegas public library, 1946. Courtesy Las Vegas–Clark County Library District.

CHAPTER FOUR

Washoe County

THE LIBRARIES OF RENO

The Washoe County Public Library System, the descendent of the Reno public library opened in 1904, is Nevada's oldest. Even after the legislative hurdles of the 1890s (discussed above) had been overcome, Frank Norcross and his hometown allies faced formidable obstacles before Reno residents could borrow books from the shelves of their own public library.[1]

Reno was a city as ambivalent about its future in 1900 as it would be in 2000. On the one hand it was Nevada's premier commercial center, with forty-five hundred people, a busy railroad depot, and a fledgling university on the hill a mile to the north. Even though it still flouted its status as a tough frontier railroad town (only thirty-one years old), it already had pretensions to becoming a cultural center.

A significant coterie of bookish women had assembled in Reno in the 1890s, eager to cultivate literary tastes across the gender barrier.[2] The possibility of the franchise for women seemed remote at that time, but people like Elizabeth Babcock, Hannah Keziah Clapp, Gertrude and Anne Martin, and Mila Tupper Maynard, among others, provided a ready-made constituency for the arguments about the educational value of a public library.

There had been a few false starts in library building in Reno before Norcross began his efforts. On several occasions during the

1880s residents of Reno had established reading clubs or library associations, but these failed. The Masonic lodge gathered a selection of books for its members as early as 1881; a group of businessmen established a literary society in 1887.[3] A decade later volunteers opened a reading room, but they were stymied when they tried to arrange the kind of funding envisioned by the statutes of 1895 and 1897. Their petition for a free public library in 1901 was rejected by county commissioners, who simply defied the law that required them to levy a small tax for libraries once they had received a petition.[4]

Thanks to the persistence of Norcross, library backers got yet another change in the library law in 1901. The new legislation empowered a district judge in a county of more than seven thousand people (Washoe was alone in that category) to certify the validity of the signatures on a library petition, authorized the state board of education to appoint a library board, and mandated that the county commissioners impose a tax within ten days thereafter.[5]

Thus Reno book lovers managed to mount the first successful Nevada experiment in building a tax-supported public library. On November 27, 1902, Norcross was elected chairman of the first library board of trustees—an appropriate choice; he not only had prepared the request to Carnegie for $15,000 but had also written the additional legislation, enacted in 1903, that allowed the city to accept the gift.[6] The library opened on May 31, 1904, with a collection of sixteen hundred books—an impressive number for a community of only about seven thousand residents. The *Reno Evening Gazette* called the structure "the handsomest public edifice in the city and when illuminated at night it is especially attractive."[7]

A subtle change was coming over Reno at the turn of the century; the struggle to open a free public library was only one part of a cultural awakening. The city was emerging from the economic depression and the culture poverty that had troubled the entire state. The new commercial activity was stimulated by the mining booms in Tonopah and Goldfield, and later the reclamation project on the Truckee River.

On the same day that the Carnegie library opened its doors, the first meeting of the Nevada Historical Society was held in Morrill Hall at the University of Nevada. Organized primarily through the efforts of history professor Jeanne Elizabeth Wier, this group began to draft a constitution and seek candidates for a slate of officers to guide it through the formative stages.[8] Three or four more years passed before the society was able to collect documents and lay the foundation of a library of its own.

The individual most responsible for organizing and cataloging the original book collection at the Reno Carnegie library was John Hamlin, who served as librarian from 1904 until 1914. Donated books were accepted and stored in the basement of the Riverside Hotel while the Carnegie building was under construction. Nearly three decades later Hamlin recalled the challenges he faced:

> No one, who is unfamiliar with the preparation of books for library usage, can have the remotest idea of the task which confronted me. Especially since I was totally ignorant of cataloging, accessioning, marking books, classifying them. Naturally I was pretty much in a panic. I wrote to the American Library Association, to numerous librarians and visited the University library. I next appealed to the trustees for an assistant to help achieve order where chaos reigned. Miss Irene Barkley, a niece of Mr. Norcross, was given the job. Together we worked in the Riverside basement every day in the week and for 12 hours at a stretch.[9]

In library service, buying the books and putting them on the shelves is less than half the job. Cataloging and making them readily accessible to patrons is the "science" part of library science. In Hamlin's time it was a tedious, time-consuming task that each library had to perform anew. He learned his vocation by trial and error.

The Carnegie library served patrons for twenty-five years; by 1928 it was overcrowded with twelve thousand volumes. The staff had established small outlets elsewhere in the Truckee Meadows, initiating the policy of outreach that later became standard. Relief from the immediate book congestion was in sight, however, because across the street to the south in Powning Park a new, stucco-covered structure was built to serve as a combined civic auditorium and community center. Generally known as the State Building, it had been constructed for an exposition in 1927 to celebrate the completion of the first transcontinental highway. Space was provided for the library (which was moved in January 1930) on the ground floor and for the Nevada Historical Society collection in the basement. At that time the library claimed to own twenty-two thousand volumes; the new quarters had space for fifty-five thousand.

Before 1929, the library had operated as a unit of the Reno school district—a somewhat larger area than the municipality—and its free services were technically available only to residents of that area. In 1929, the legislature enacted two laws, proposed by Assemblyman Ed Mulcahy of Sparks, creating a county library board for Washoe County and granting it expanded authority managing library affairs.[10] Mulcahy's activity reflected a growing community interest in establishing a separate library in Sparks. This was finally accomplished in 1932.

From 1914 until 1941, Henry W. Miles was a key library employee of the Reno library. He was an assistant during the first seven years and head librarian through the 1920s and 1930s. During the Great Depression, the library saw a substantial increase in usage at the same time it suffered severe cuts in its budget. Like many public employees Miles and his assistants faced reductions in pay as their work load increased. Miles initiated a radio book review program in 1933 and a film forum, as well as regular literary meetings.

In 1940, Edwin Castagna joined the staff; he succeeded Miles as head librarian the following year, and the innovations in service accelerated. He added a phonograph record collection in 1941 to serve music lovers and acquired a former ambulance in 1947 to serve as the first bookmobile in the state.

Washoe libraries marked time during World War II and the early postwar era. By the time Schenk wrote her report in 1958, the main library in the State Building and the Sparks branch had acute problems. The collections, wrote Schenk, had been handled with "care and resourcefulness in spite of extreme overcrowding, especially in the main library. The (State) building is no longer adequate to provide full scale service either to the City of Reno or the County of Washoe."[11]

By the early 1960s, the effects of the "thirty-year cycle" on the Reno library in the State Building were evident. Fortunately the Fleischmann Foundation was on the scene by that time, and Washoe County was the first recipient of its largess. After a long delay caused by controversy over where the new library should be located, the trustees settled on the site at 301 South Center Street, just two blocks south of the State Building. For better or worse the thirty years had stretched out to thirty-five, and the library was still located in the center of Reno. The site was convenient, but downtown parking was increasingly a problem for patrons.

The $1.2 million building, dedicated on May 22, 1966, was a marvel of architectural design produced by Hewitt Wells of Reno. Its glass front and interior open space filled with mature trees and a hanging garden won several national awards. The combination of circular stairways connecting four levels and a circular reference desk were striking features. It had more than three times as much space for the collection—forty thousand square feet, compared to twelve thousand in the State Building.[12]

William Andrews was director when the library staff took possession of the Fleischmann building. He defined the role of the library as being not only a circulator and custodian of books but also a cultural center. It included a 106-seat auditorium for concerts and meetings, available free of charge. When the new facility opened, the system claimed 143,000 volumes; it doubled its collection to 300,000 in the next thirteen years.[13]

Andrews retired as director of the library in 1979. By the time of his departure, the system had been expanded to include the Sparks library (see below) and branches in the senior citizen center on East Ninth Street, at Incline Village (with help from the Fleischmann Foundation), and at Stead, which operated in cooperation with the community college.

Andrews's replacement was Frank Virostek, who served in the early 1980s. During his tenure, the state and local governments faced their first major shortfall in tax revenue in forty years. When administrators were forced to make budget cuts, libraries were among the first institutions to be hit. Washoe libraries lost authorized positions, reluctantly reduced hours of access, trimmed budgets for books and periodicals, and sharply curtailed technical services and programs for children. Plans for outreach and expansion were placed in limbo.

Martha Gould, a former employee of the state library, had joined the staff as public service librarian in 1974. She served as acting director on two occasions, finally becoming director in August 1984 at a time when the library was reeling from heavy budget cuts. A forceful and articulate administrator, Gould became a persistent advocate for improved support during her ten-year term as head of the system, but the challenges were formidable.

When the state's voters had approved the $10 million bond issue for libraries in 1984, Washoe librarians expected to obtain $2.3 million to meet their growing needs, based on population figures. When the distribution was made by the Interim Finance Committee in 1986, however, Washoe's libraries received only $99,000—less than 1 percent—because the county had only a

small tax base with which to generate the matching money required by the formula developed by the legislature.[14] Clark
County, which had a large independent tax base for libraries and
which had recently approved a $15 million bond issue for libraries,
received more than $7 million, and several rural districts also
benefitted.

Gould and her staff struggled on, gradually increasing local
awareness of the library's acute needs. A candid 260-page Citizens'
Blue Ribbon Advisory Committee report prepared early in
Gould's term documented the previous neglect of the Washoe library system and made a strong case for more and better service.
Issued in 1987, the report called for the restoration of services that
had been cut, the opening of new branches, and the improvement
of databases. It marshaled impressive arguments and evidence
about the needs of a growing community in the rapidly changing
world of libraries.[15]

Gould and Joyce Ball of the University of Nevada, Reno, had
laid the groundwork for an automated system in 1976–1978; they
established close cooperation in building a database. Computers
were housed at the university, with much of the funding and staff
support coming from federal, state, and Washoe County funds.
This arrangement continued until the late 1980s, when the university installed a different computer system.

From 1960 until the late 1970s, the Washoe library system operated bookmobiles to serve outlying areas, including towns in
Storey, Lyon, and Churchill Counties. This proved to be a popular
but costly undertaking, and by 1980 Gould and her staff had
phased out this program. The last bookmobile served Gerlach in
northern Washoe County and was replaced by a "partnership library" at the high school. Other sites for partnership libraries were
developed with schools at Billinghurst, Galena, Mendive, Traner-
Duncan, and Verdi. Branches also were established or expanded at
Sierra View and North Valleys/Peavine. The Sierra View branch,
opened in 1987, was located in spacious quarters in Old Town Mall

in south Reno and quickly became one of the most popular branches in the system. It shares space with the regional literacy center, which offers tutoring to those who have difficulty reading.

The Washoe library system suffered once again from a financial crisis in the early 1990s, forced this time by a legislative decision to shift state-support funds from northern to southern Nevada. This so-called "fair share" redistribution was based on a finding that Clark County had been receiving less per capita from state funds than Washoe.[16] In 1994 the organizational structure of the system called for 108 staff positions in the system, but only enough money was available to employ 94.

Gould, the staff, and the board faced the challenges of the early 1990s with unprecedented energy. They gradually built community support for a new method of funding, cushioned from the vicissitudes of politics and fluctuating revenues. Relief for the beleaguered system finally came in 1994 when the library community asked the voters to add a two-cent "tax override" on the existing level of property taxes. The voters narrowly approved the measure, assuring the system of approximately $1.1 million annually for the next thirty years. It thus became possible to restore most of the services that had been reduced in the early 1980s, to implement better acquisitions budgets, and to improve Internet access.

The Blue Ribbon report of 1987 had called for a new full-service library in the northwest Truckee Meadows by 1991. This did not happen until 1999, when a building near Robb Drive donated by Jack Tranor was redesigned for library use. It was the first new full-service library building opened in the greater Reno area since the completion of the downtown Fleischmann library in 1966 and was the result of a unique agreement between private donors and public resources—a lease-purchase arrangement that saved the system much money. The northwest library has a stunning view of the valley and substantial room for growth.

In the meantime the much admired downtown main library

was falling victim to the "thirty-year cycle." Still regarded as an architectural marvel, its effectiveness as a library in the electronic age was questionable. Designed before the era of computers, it required continuous retrofitting. This became a major concern of the new leadership of the 1990s.

Nancy Cummings, who had previously served libraries in Yuma and Las Vegas, became director of the system in 1994 and guided it through the more promising years of the late 1990s. Voter approval of the tax override and obvious public support for an expanding system gave library patrons and the staff reason for optimism for the first time in decades. The partnership program was expanding, not only with schools but also with social service organizations, and a new bookmobile service was planned to begin in 2000. The Washoe system received attention for its resourceful work in giving access to patrons through new electronic media—a "branch library in cyberspace."

Through all the transitions that occurred in the last decades of the 1900s, the Washoe system had the invaluable services of a dedicated staff, of whom Associate Director Charles Manley was a central figure, and an activist, supportive board of trustees and friends' group. It was a highly successful community enterprise.

SPARKS

Meanwhile Sparks, the division point on the Southern Pacific Railroad, had a library history of its own stretching back almost to the beginning of the twentieth century. Soon after the town arose in 1904, a small railroad library was established and fitted up "in style,"[17] but it was destroyed by fire in July 1908.[18] The library was not replaced for more than two decades, when another community effort emerged.

When the original Carnegie building in downtown Reno was

about to be vacated in 1929, county commissioners considered moving it to Sparks, but it was too fragile and the project too costly for that solution to be practical. Also, the more vocal citizens of Sparks wanted their own new building.

The Sparks library movement of 1929 originated with parents convinced that local school libraries were inadequate for the needs of their children. They persuaded the 1931 session of the legislature to authorize a $25,000 bond issue for construction of a library, which opened at a central location on B Street on January 1, 1932.[19]

The "thirty-year cycle" occurred also in Sparks. By the 1960s the B Street edifice that had been a source of pride during the Great Depression and World War II was no longer adequate. The circulation of books had increased fourfold in the 1950s alone, and shelves were bulging. The Sparks delegation to the legislature in 1963 managed to enact a $250,000 authorization for library bonds to construct a replacement building.

The new building opened on February 27, 1965, at Oddie Boulevard and 12th Street, nearer the population center of the expanding municipality. Thus it went into service more than a year before the new Fleischmann building in Reno was ready. Sparks received significant support from local civic groups and became eligible for federal money soon after the new facility began operating.

In Sparks as in other growing urban areas, the "thirty-year cycle" shortened in the last quarter of the century. The book holdings doubled in less than fifteen years, and the number of patrons increased to challenge the capacity of the 1965 building. Responding to public pressure in April 1980, the county commissioners approved a $700,000 expansion that would provide another twelve thousand square feet of new space.[20] Yet another enlargement project in 1987 provided more space for children.

Fortunes can change rapidly in the realm of public services. Sparks book lovers had a fright in 1984 when, as a result of the economic recession and a shortfall in tax revenues, the Washoe County library board of trustees considered a proposal that this branch be closed to save money.[21] It was argued that the thirteen staff members then employed in Sparks could be shifted to Reno. When Gould assumed the post as library board director, this contingency was avoided and all branches curtailed their hours of service. The crisis passed, and the following year it was possible to expand hours of service again.

CHAPTER FIVE

Fifteen Counties
A Panorama

Nevada has long been regarded by insiders as having three subcultures: Washoe County; the fifteen counties that were sufficiently beyond the burgeoning commercial centers to maintain their special identities; and Clark County, the late-blooming giant in the Sunbelt.

In the hundred thousand square miles beyond Reno, the social energy to establish public libraries emerged slowly. "The biggest little city in the world" was the largest community in the state and held this status until the mid-1950s. Norcross, the prime mover of Reno's library movement, was a respected attorney, a graduate of the first class of the University of Nevada in 1891. He had the legal skills and the connections of a pioneering family in the male-dominated society to give substance to his dream on the banks of the Truckee River.

Elsewhere in Nevada, the task was more difficult; nearly all the libraries were established through the initiative and the volunteer service of women, who worked tirelessly to convince often skeptical local governing boards that even a remote country town needed and deserved a collection of books, supported by public funds, to nourish their children and bring enlightenment to those who wanted an alternative to the temptations of the mining and railroad towns. Nevada had a population of only 42,335 in 1900 and 110,247 forty years later.

In 1905, when Mabel Prentiss, a California library promoter, arrived in Reno to try to organize the professional librarians of Nevada into an association, she found no candidates for her movement. California had more than a hundred public libraries at that time; Nevada had the one tender institution newly established in Reno and another about to be opened in Tonopah.[1] Another four decades passed before Nevada was ready for a formal association of librarians.

During this period, Nevada was predominantly a man's state, with the population of men outnumbering women by as much as two-to-one in many of the rural counties. The miners, ranchers, cowboys, and railroad crews that constituted much of the labor force had precious little time for, even if they had an interest in, bookish matters.

The women were only marginally better off. Historian Joanne Passet has suggested that throughout the Far West, the mundane duties of maintaining a home and the basic requirements of coping with chores discouraged women of all but the most privileged classes even from forming the social improvement groups that later became prominent.[2] Anita Watson, in her admirable study of the empowerment of Nevada women, has chronicled the difficult rise of clubs devoted to social services in the first two decades of the century.[3]

Between 1905 and 1940, citizens in small towns laid the foundations for thirteen public libraries. Reno's was the most prominent because of the enterprise of Norcross and largest of the Carnegie gift. Elsewhere, local governments eventually gave modest support to institutions founded by volunteers—nearly always women. The following list gives the dates of their founding or the beginning of local government assistance:

Tonopah, 1905
Wells, 1914
Las Vegas, 1916
White Pine (Ely), 1916

Fallon, 1918(?)
Lovelock, 1919
Yerington, 1921
Elko, 1922
Winnemucca, 1923
Sparks, 1933
Boulder City, 1937
Lincoln County (Pioche), 1929(?)–1938

The remainder of this chapter surveys the histories of the most interesting of them, not in chronological order but according to a roughly regional pattern.

NYE COUNTY

We begin with sprawling Nye County because of its size and the remarkable diversity of its experiments and because Tonopah has the second-oldest public library, which remained in 2000 a venerable exhibit of the frontier values. Within its eighteen thousand square miles Nye has six distinct libraries within five separate districts, as different from one another as the variegated landscape of central Nevada will allow.

Tonopah, the premier silver-mining camp of the twentieth century, takes pride in having the oldest public library building still in service in Nevada. Only two years after silver ore was discovered in 1900, the town received a gift of one hundred classic and contemporary volumes from George Weeks of Alameda, California, who donated the books in memory of a brother who had recently died in Tonopah.[4] It may be presumed that the deceased brother had hauled the books to Tonopah during the silver rush, and the benefactor had no way to take possession.

While Weeks's gift did not immediately generate a public library, the inspiration for such a venture was revived a few years later by a group of women led by Grace R. (Mrs. Hugh) Brown, a lady with genteel social values who later wrote a colorful memoir of her experiences.[5] She led a town meeting on Thanksgiving Day 1904 to discuss the possibility of a library. Soon a building site was donated by the Tonopah Mining Company, and cash arrived from businessmen and other citizens. A small but durable stone building was erected in 1905 and was occupied in January 1906. The company provided financial support until 1917, long after its operations were profitable. Subsequently the Nye County commissioners assumed responsibility.

The one-room structure, only thirty-eight feet long and twenty-eight feet wide, was still in service ninety-five years later, virtually unchanged from the time of its founding except for a few elementary plumbing and electrical modifications. No other town in the state has made such a shrine of its original library building; present and past residents of Tonopah often offer nostalgic testimonials to its cozy solace. In 2000 it was still crammed with shelves and furniture, some dating from the bonanza days before 1910. It welcomed children with its rustic decor, and the screened front porch has been seen heaped with books discarded and donated, available for the taking. It was a symbol of the pioneering spirit of library development a century ago.

In 1990 the library received a gift for a $140,553 from Mrs. Eleanor Gavrilovich to provide either for an enlargement or new quarters.[6] Additional money has since been offered at times from the state level. Tonopah citizens, however, did not reach a consensus for several years about whether to replace the old building, construct an addition, or incorporate everything in a new and larger structure. The result was inaction until 2000, when an addition adjacent to the original structure was placed in service. In a community that has built a fine local mining museum from the artifacts of the past, the old library itself was a relic, more dedicated to sentiment than to current library science.

Nye County's other six libraries are distant from the county seat; they have resisted the kind of consolidation that all other rural counties have adopted. Separate collections are available in

Amargosa Valley, Beatty, Gabbs, Pahrump, Round Mountain, and Manhattan, all supported by the local constituency. The latter two have merged in a district known as Smoky Valley; each of the other four has a separate library district. This arrangement reflects the spirit of local sovereignty in Nye County. In the 1980s a state-of-the-art facility was built at Round Mountain after years of fund-raising, organizing, and lobbying before the Nevada Council on Libraries by Keith Lyon and other tenacious local boosters.

In 1973, Dorothy Shirkey of Pahrump, following the advice of a statewide survey, proposed that Nye County establish a single library district. The county commissioners, noted for many years for their opposition to any guidance or control from the state or national level, rejected the idea on the grounds that library development was a matter for individual towns. Because Pahrump was much nearer to Las Vegas than to the unresponsive "county dads" in Tonopah, its citizens sought bookmobile service from Clark County and quickly proved to be among the most zealous borrowers in southern Nevada. In 1976, a committee of women headed by Shirkey took over an old municipal court building and started their own book collection. They formed a district in 1979 and founded a five-thousand-square-foot library, which they named for Shirkey.[7] In the next twenty years, this virtual suburb of Las Vegas grew to twenty-seven thousand citizens, and the library was suffocating for lack of space, even though it had moved into an abandoned casino.

In the 1990s, a dynamic group of enthusiasts found two acres of free land and proposed a $3 million bond issue to give the library an elegant home in a setting that featured the latest amenities in parking, computers, and social conveniences against a backdrop of Mount Charleston. The voters approved the bond issue in September 1998. "If we can do it, anyone can," library director Charlene Board told the NLA meeting in Elko in 1999. The new, "cathedral-like" facility opened in 2001.

The library at Gabbs is another model of what an isolated small-town oasis of books can become, but here a more gradual path was followed.[8] The town was founded during World War II to serve the families of workers employed in the magnesite and brucite mines—strategic minerals desperately needed for the defense industries. Within a few months of its beginning, the Gabbs Women's Club formed the nucleus of a library (1943). Fifty-five years later, three of the founders were still providing the volunteer service that has sustained the facility throughout its history. They have been able to build support from local, state, and national governments and funding from private sources that could make library boosters elsewhere envious. Even as the mining industry declined, dedication to the library endured.

A private library from the beginning, the Gabbs facility relied upon donated space and had to move several times. In 1960 it found its permanent home when Basic Inc., the town's main employer, contributed a structure adjacent to the schoolhouse. Twice in the last four decades the library's friends have found it necessary and possible to expand the building; local private giving has been remarkable. Upon the death of Barbara Gates, one of the institution's most ardent supporters, friends advanced a substantial amount in her memory. The women made arrangements to provide library service to the schoolchildren and generated assistance from the school board.

Gabbs was the only incorporated city in Nye County during the late 1900s. In 1978 the women's club, by then thirty-five years old, asked the municipal government to take ownership of the library so it could apply for a Fleischmann Foundation grant. It received $60,000 from that source for an enlargement of its space.

Margaret Jones, who was the acknowledged leader of the efforts on behalf of the library, and her allies gathered financial support from many sources on a regular basis and built one of the finest rural collections in a spacious facility. The ladies of Gabbs are justly proud of their achievement and especially their collection of Nevadiana.

WHITE PINE

The White Pine copper mining boom of the early twentieth century provided the backdrop for a library in Ely in 1916. The vast ore body was discovered at Ruth in 1900, and the smelter to process the ore arose at McGill. Halfway between the two industrial sites was Ely, the pastoral survivor of an earlier mining era, which became the county seat and cultural center for the region. It was the strategic place for a library, when the spirit moved its citizens.

This venture began, as usual, at the grass roots when the Women's Club of Ely presented a petition to the county commissioners asking for $300 to buy books and another $300 in monthly installments to maintain the collection. The commissioners looked favorably on the first request but did not approve of the second; care of the volumes seemed a dubious expenditure of public funds.[9] Members of the Women's Club had the help of the mayor in collecting another $300 and were able to buy more books; they opened the free public library in late June 1916 in the White Pine County high school. They found a recent graduate of the University of Nevada, Dorothy Parker, to serve as their volunteer librarian.[10]

The founders had difficulty from the beginning in providing service, dependent as they were on volunteers. The city of Ely and the Nevada Consolidated Copper Company added modest support to the earlier contributions, and within a year the women had rented rooms in the local power and light building near the railroad depot. After persuading the county to increase its ante, they hired Parker at a modest wage.[11]

In Ely as elsewhere, pulling support from the local governments was a slow, tedious process. The Women's Club worked for months to get continuing commitments and cash from the Ely city government and additional help from the county. The library acquired space in the Ely fire station in 1929, where the collection remained for four decades.

The situation changed little for more than forty years. In 1970, with a gift of $188,000 from the Fleischmann Foundation, a grant of $155,000 from the federal Library Services and Construction Act, and $10,000 from the county government, the community got an 8,400-square-foot facility with many of the technical and spacial resources of a contemporary library.[12] It was still serving the community well after three decades of use.

ELKO AND ITS NEIGHBORS

Elko County was established in 1869 when the building of the Central Pacific Railroad opened the expansive rangelands to the livestock business. It had high cultural aspirations almost from the beginning and is proud of its heritage as a pioneering community in educational matters in eastern Nevada. Elko was the first home of the University Preparatory School (1874–1885) and the founder of the community college movement in Nevada (1968). Elko also formed one of Nevada's earliest community-based libraries, which celebrated its seventy-fifth anniversary in 1997.[13]

In 1922, women of the Twentieth Century Club began to collect and catalog books for public use. Acquiring a room in the courthouse, they opened their library on January 31, 1922, with four volunteers. This was their home for four years, until they were forced to move to a former high school building (later sometimes called the American Legion Hall) nearby. These makeshift quarters served for another sixteen years—from 1926 until 1942—until a fire destroyed many books and much newly acquired furniture. (Most financial support for the improvements had come from food sales, dinners, and dances sponsored by women's groups.) Some volumes, however, escaped the flames and were moved into a lodge hall to form the basis of later collections.

The Elko librarians expanded their services to outlying communities in the 1950s and 1960s, reaching Jackpot, Montello, Owyhee, and Tuscarora. In the mid-1960s, responding to the 1965 law authorizing intercounty library districts, Elko library administrators arranged to offer services to their co-workers in Lander and Eureka Counties. Through the initiative of Governor Mike O'Callaghan, the state provided three bookmobiles. This outreach was a result of the growing spirit of cooperation evident in most parts of the state.

Mrs. Ruthe Gallagher, a dedicated leader of the library trustees in the 1960s, proposed a new building program for Elko in that decade but could not arouse the necessary level of local support. In 1969, Hailie Tomingas Gunn became director of the library and took a leadership role in the Nevada Library Association. She held the major responsibilities for seeking the Fleischmann grant, pooling it with local contributions and funds from the Library Services and Construction Act of 1964 and putting them to work. The result was a $563,619 commitment to the construction of a new building. The modern library at 720 Court Street, designed to hold fifty thousand volumes, was dedicated on April 27, 1974. For more than twenty-five years it has been a community center as well as a depository of books and a window on the world. It has a conference room, kitchen facilities, and a much-used young people's department. The Elko library began to develop a reference department in 1976 and hired its first children's librarian in 1977. A large addition for children's services opened in 1987 with help from federal, state, and local sources.

Elko has become the hub and central resource for libraries, as well as for community college education, in much of north-central Nevada.

Eureka, one of the silver boomtowns of the 1870s, dwindled to a few hundred people during the depression years but has traditionally been one of the more progressive small towns in the state. It mustered enough civic pride in the 1970s and 1980s to seek and obtain two Fleischmann grants totaling $130,000. This institution, like its Lander County neighbors Austin and Battle Mountain, benefitted from regional cooperation with Elko County in a three-county library system with headquarters in Elko.

Wells can claim one of the earliest public libraries in the state, four or five years older than its sibling in Elko, because the members of the Home Makers' Club in that small railroad town assembled their first collection of books in 1914 or 1915. Yet it had a more troubled and impoverished life, despite the continuing support from the Home Makers, because it was not a county seat. It did not have adequate quarters until it moved into a new municipal building on south Clover Avenue in 1960. Its merger with the other northeastern libraries in the 1970s significantly enhanced its services, and state bond money provided a new building in the 1980s.

HUMBOLDT COUNTY

Early efforts to operate a reading club were also recorded in Winnemucca.[14] One of the original railroad towns along the route of the Central Pacific, it was founded in 1868; by 1871 it had a fraternal order that announced a reading room for its members. In 1880 women of the community took over a building formerly used as a furniture store, acquired assorted volumes, and heralded a grand opening on October 23. The books of this library were available only to those who paid monthly dues, but it was open nearly every evening. This institution seems to have existed for about seven years. The collection was given to the Winnemucca school district in 1887. Another unsuccessful effort to establish a library is recorded in 1903.

Citizens of Winnemucca had their first success in forming a public library in 1923 through the efforts of a newly founded Civic Club, which held a "grand opening" with a tea and entertainment on February 6, 1923. By April the club announced that it had purchased 175 books and that another 65 had been donated.[15] It was staffed by volunteers for the first five years; they found space for their books in a business building.

It was a Winnemucca resident, Mary G. Rose, one of the first women elected to the state assembly, who in 1925 introduced the landmark bill authorizing county commissioners to set aside $1,500 annually for the operation and maintenance of a free county library. This bill, enacted near the end of the session and signed by Governor James G. Scrugham, provided also for the appointment by school boards of a library board of trustees.[16] This became another foundation stone in erecting a system of public libraries built from the grass roots.

The Humboldt County commissioners moved slowly, however, appropriating only $250 in June 1926 for library purposes. The library was closed for several months, until December 1926, when the commissioners agreed to pay the salary of a librarian. It became the practice to ask the patrons to contribute five cents for each twenty-four books they borrowed. As usual, the original library was housed in inadequate quarters; when the collection grew to three thousand volumes, a change of location became necessary. In the late 1920s the library was moved into the courthouse.

The 1956 federal Library Service Act (LSA) stimulated activity in Winnemucca as it did in many other parts of the state. The Winnemucca public library evolved into the Humboldt County Library, and the trustees oversaw an extensive remodelling of the courthouse room. By 1967 the county had engaged its first full-time librarian, Rosemary Miller, who combined a Fleischmann grant, federal funds, and locally raised friends' contributions for a new building. This structure, costing nearly $250,000, opened in January 1968. During this era Miller and her associates established four branch libraries and initiated bookmobile services to remote areas.

Mrs. Miller's successor, Sharon "Sheri" Allen, has served for three decades, becoming one of the ranking members of the

Nevada library profession. Early in her tenure the Humboldt library added and furnished a separate children's library with the assistance of the Humboldt County Fair and Recreation Board. The library underwent a substantial expansion in the 1990s. It now has branches in McDermitt and Denio.

PERSHING COUNTY — LOVELOCK

The library at Lovelock appeared about a decade after the town became the seat of newly created Pershing County in 1919. Earlier the local high school gave borrowing privileges to nonstudents one afternoon a week. The Lion's Club took the initiative, opening the first public library on June 20, 1930. It had 240 volumes and was housed in the basement of the courthouse.[17] These quarters served book users for the next forty years—until 1970. The federal Works Progress Administration provided funds to pay a librarian in the 1930s, and after 1935 the county commissioners authorized a small budget.

Serious thinking about a new home began in 1957, when local residents met with state librarian Joseph Schubert; a Friends of the Library group was organized early in 1958. The board of trustees began detailed planning in 1966 with the prospect of money from federal sources and the Fleischmann Foundation. Eventually the board received $79,482 from the foundation, $47,683 in federal grants, and $1,650 from the Friends of the Library. The planners selected a location across the street north of the courthouse for a 3,800-square-foot building designed to hold ten thousand volumes. They broke ground in August 1969 and transferred books into the attractive structure in 1970.

Within fifteen years, the collection grew far beyond the capacity of the new facility, exceeding seventeen thousand volumes by the mid-1980s. When local government authorities placed the question of a $260,000 bond issue on the ballot, it won approval.

Pershing County qualified for $48,500 from the $10 million state fund authorized by the voters in 1984, which allowed for a new addition opened in 1987. Before the passage of the bond issue, county commissioners had been parsimonious in allotting money to the library purposes, but since 1990, with increasing use of the expanded facilities, they have become more generous.

CHURCHILL COUNTY — FALLON

Fallon began to emerge as a town soon after the Newlands Project legislation of 1903 generated federal money for reclamation. It had a post office by 1905 when it was still a tent city. The postmistress established a small lending library as an added public service.[18] Although several early attempts were made to found reading rooms and lending societies, the first to succeed was a literary club called the Draper Group, which borrowed a room in the Methodist Church in 1918. Women volunteers performed the usual chores for several years; county commissioners began to provide a regular budget in 1925.

The collection was relocated several times before settling in a former doctor's office on South Maine Street in 1932. Although the collection was small, it was not finally cataloged until 1957.

Dora Witt, who became librarian in 1960, led a movement to arouse community support. After forming a Friends of the Library group she prepared a request to the Fleischmann Foundation in 1966. Her efforts brought a grant of $111,208, which when supplemented by $65,118 from the federal government, $16,470 from the county, and $3,156 from local contributions, provided for the first adequate space for books and library activities.

The new 9,300-square-foot building at 553 South Maine Street became the library's home on April 15, 1967. It has served the county well thirty-three years, despite that fact that, having been designed for twenty thousand volumes, it contained a collection

three times that size in 1999 under the direction of Barbara
Mathews. It assists students at the Fallon branch of the Western
Nevada Community College and personnel at the nearby naval air
station as well as the usual community patrons.

LYON COUNTY

As early as 1907, the women's book club of Yerington tried to
form a reading club for children who, upon graduating from the
eighth grade, had no local possibility for further study, since the
town did not yet have a high school. In 1908 they established a
reading room in a local bank building, hoping to encourage their
young people to continue regular reading. When a proposal for a
high school appeared on the ballot the following year, they urged
that a library be included, to no avail. This failed: The school was
approved in a 1909 bond election—but without plans for a library.
The reading room functioned for about a year, then the sixty or so
books were placed in storage until a library could be provided.[19]

Yerington got its first regular library in 1921 when the Farm
Bureau, the Parent-Teachers' Association, and the Yerington Women's Club joined hands to gather books. An employee of the Agricultural Extension Service persuaded the University of Nevada
to lend a few books for the cause. The Farm Bureau office provided the first housing for the collection. Subsequently the county
commissioners agreed to pay $15 for rent and $50 in wages for a
librarian each month during the 1920s.

Library devotees saw their facility moved two or three times
during the next quarter century, but no significant improvement
in its housing occurred until the 1970s. The county commissioners
helped the library board obtain a site on Nevin Way early in the
1970s, and the board was allowed to hire an architect to take advantage of funds available from the Fleischmann Foundation
(which granted $225,000) and from the federal government

($123,043). The county provided more than $100,000 for site preparation, labor, and supplies. The new building, which incorporated the basic Fleischmann design, was dedicated on August 14, 1976. A Friends of the Library society bolstered the resources with luncheons, book sales, recycling of aluminum cans, and similar activities.

As the new building in Yerington was being planned in 1973, two women volunteered to start a branch in a dilapidated former town hall in Fernley, and the typical cycle began once more. Within three years a small but new library building had been constructed in this Newlands Reclamations Project community near Interstate 80; the founders opened its doors before the main library in Yerington was ready for service, partly with state bond money.

By 1981, the county was ready to support a branch in the sprawling town of Silver Springs on Highway 50 at a location called Stagecoach. Near the center of the community, it began serving its neighborhood almost immediately with more than four thousand books cataloged in Yerington and with the help of state bond money. Four years later, in October 1985, volunteers acquired the books and amenities to furnish a branch in Smith Valley, and named the facility the Ida Compston Library in Wellington. There is also a branch in Dayton Valley, which moved from a store front into its own building in January 1997.

LINCOLN COUNTY

The last public library to gain local government support before World War II was in Lincoln County. Pioche, the isolated mining camp 175 miles north of Las Vegas, had been founded during the winter of 1869–1870; it prospered on silver production for about five years, then endured the typical decline that was the fate of all the bonanza-era towns. The town had a private circulating library as early as 1872, operated by the Weiderhold Pioneering News Depot. The proprietor charged a rental fee of twenty-five cents per volume.[20] After the boom peaked in the mid-1870s the economy plummeted and the Weiderhold venture faded with the hopes of the camp. For fifty years Pioche languished in the economic doldrums.

A daughter-in-law of Weiderhold, Louise Thompson, led the movement for a town library in the late 1920s. She and her friend Florence Thomas rallied other bookish women in the enterprise. Pioche was undergoing a reawakening in those years based on the testing of lead-zinc ores, a revival that continued into the 1930s despite the Great Depression. Eventually Mrs. Thompson and Mrs. Thomas were joined by the Women's Auxiliary of Mining and Metallurgical Engineers, who donated books solicited from across the country. The first library opened in the Scott building, one of the venerable brick survivals of the bonanza era. In about 1929 the library was moved to a small frame structure on upper Main Street.

Their collection became a county library in about 1938 when county commissioners came to their assistance. By the mid-1940s, this one-room haven was bulging with nearly two thousand books. Like so many sibling institutions, it was inadequate for even the small population it was expected to serve—about four thousand people scattered over the ten thousand square miles of Lincoln County. In 1960, James Gottfredson, a Caliente businessman, donated a much larger building on Main Street in Pioche, a former hardware store, for library and museum purposes. Later it moved once more to a former meat market, also on Main Street.

Even so, the problem of serving the county's scattered population remained. The library district inherited an old potato chip truck, which rambled over the roads for several years in the 1980s until it became unreliable. In 1990 Jean L. Breautigam, who had made her home in the county for health reasons, saw a tin cup in the Pioche library asking for donations to help buy a bookmobile. She contributed enough money to purchase a new vehicle.[21]

Twenty-five miles south of Pioche, the railroad town of Caliente also had a local voluntary library as early as the 1930s, founded by Hazel B. Denton, a local schoolteacher who was later elected to the legislature. The local school board supported the effort for several years. No county-supported institution has been identified before 1965, when Caliente united with the county library system at Pioche and occupied an old jewelry store.

In 1975, Caliente's librarians got access to part of the former Union Pacific Railroad depot, a handsome mission revival structure listed on the National Register of Historic Places. In the 1990s, they received substantial gifts from the Union Pacific to assist with their efforts. In the early 1980s Lincoln County opened a branch in Alamo to serve the Pahranagat Valley, fifty miles south of Caliente.

LATER LIBRARIES OF NORTHERN NEVADA
Ormsby County—Carson City

Because the people of Ormsby County had borrowing privileges at the state library since the 1890s, they saw no need for a local library until the state was forced to end its liberal lending policy in 1966. Soon after Mildred Heyer announced the change in 1965, the county commissioners appointed the first board of library trustees, and a friends' organization was formed.

The basement of a former civic auditorium on Carson Street was selected as the first home for an assortment of donated books and volumes lent from the state library. The typical scenario followed; the space became inadequate within three years as the collection expanded. The board and friends then turned to the Fleischmann Foundation (which had also contributed to early book purchases) and to federal sources for help in financing a new building. Construction began on a 13,600-square-foot building at a site on North Roop and East Washington Streets late in 1970. This structure opened on May 10, 1971, when the population of the state capital was about ten thousand.

Within ten years the number of residents had tripled, and space was again inadequate. Library trustees approached the Fleischmann board a second time, and in 1980, shortly before it disbanded, the foundation provided most of the funding for an 8,000-square-foot addition. By the late 1990s, with the population of Carson City approaching fifty thousand, this was one of the most overcrowded libraries in the state. On some days the number of patrons exceeded three thousand.

In 1998 the trustees turned to the voters, asking for authority to add a five-cent-per-year property tax "override" on each $100 of assessed valuation—an amount estimated to cost the average household about $17.50 per year, or slightly less than a nickel a day. The additional revenue would have financed longer hours and eventually an expansion of the building. Citizens for Better Libraries waged an energetic campaign, confident that voters would support their efforts, because library service was obviously highly popular. They were surprised when the override was defeated by a slim margin on election day.

Sally Edwards, the library's dedicated director, and her committed staff struggled on, providing a broad range of assistance under trying circumstances. A desperate need exists for the quiet space and working room essential for such an institution. Library personnel try to keep abreast of the expanding population by responding to special needs of senior citizens, children, professionals, and non-English speakers, among others.

Early in its history, this institution was formally named the Ormsby County Library. It retained this title even though in 1969 the separate governments of Carson City and Ormsby County were merged by the legislature. In 1991 the trustees voted to rename it the Carson City Library. This was, however, still a misnomer because thousands of clients arrive from neighboring counties—Washoe, Storey, Lyon, and Douglas—as well as from Carson City, compounding the crowding. Local government leaders were considering submitting another bond issue to the voters.

Douglas County

Although the earliest permanent settlement in Nevada was located at Genoa, Douglas County was one of the last in the state to have its own public library. The proximity of Genoa, Minden, and Gardnerville to Carson City explains the delay. The state library served many local patrons as the main source of general reading material from the turn of the century until 1965.

Wynne M. Maule, author of a useful history of Minden, identifies the first attempt to establish a library in 1933.[22] Donations of books and money facilitated the beginning of a small collection in the office of farm bureau agent in the courthouse. Twenty years later the local 20-30 Club made a similar effort to establish a local library. It did not, however, have any official status within the local government context.

In 1963 state librarian Mildred Heyer observed that Douglas was one of four counties in Nevada without a public library. The following year the Carson Valley Area Development Committee (CVAD) adopted as one of its priorities the establishment of a local public library, and other civic organizations embraced the project. At that time the county had fewer than five thousand residents.

The first efforts of the library boosters were controversial and disappointing. One stimulant for this initiative was the realization that the state library after July 1966 would no longer serve as a lending library for the citizens of the state. CVAD began to solicit donations through local service agencies and to explore the possibility of a Fleischmann Foundation grant. The management of funds and the issue of selecting a site for a new building became highly contentious, and the initial structure, built in 1966–1967, proved to be too small to accommodate the needs of Douglas County; it was overcrowded within three years. During the 1970s it was clear that Douglas County did not yet have a library worthy of its population.

In the spring of 1980, the Fleischmann Foundation came to the rescue with a grant of $900,000, part of which was to be devoted to a facility at Lake Tahoe. Prolonged discussion over where to locate a new, larger building was resolved in 1981 when various groups agreed to accept a site near Highway 88 that had been offered by Duane "Scotchy" Mack as a donation.

Mineral County—Hawthorne

For the first seventy-five years of its existence, Hawthorne had no library. Founded as a railroad town on the ill-fated Carson & Colorado in 1881, it did not enjoy either the ephemeral prosperity of the mining camps or the stability of the agricultural communities. Only after the federal Naval Ammunition Depot (NAD) was located there in 1929 did the community have a relatively fixed economic base.[23]

In 1954 the local Business and Professional Women took up the cause, refurbished a small county-owned building, gathered donated books, and began operating with volunteers. The Mineral County commissioners appointed a library board the following year. In 1961 the American Association of University Women (AAUW) persuaded the commissioners to seek an empty house at the NAD depot in Babbitt and to donate a small amount ($135) for relocating and equipping the building.

Because the Mineral County tax base was extremely small (Hawthorne is a virtual island of private property surrounded by the huge, untaxed ammunition depot), local government support was meager. The "new" library came into existence through donated labor and materials and opened on April 23, 1963. Within two years a branch had been established at Mina.

Library patronage and resources increased, and the space in the Hawthorne library had become inadequate within a decade. In 1977, when federal funds were made available to the state for library improvements, the state librarian channeled $180,000 to Hawthorne. With an additional $130,000 economic development grant from the U.S. Department of Commerce, the county was able to begin constructing its first truly new public depository for books at a spacious site at First and A Streets.

Dedicated on October 14, 1978—ninety-seven years after the founding of its host community—the Mineral County Library was worthy of comparison to the score of other attractive learning and leisure-book centers in the other small towns of Nevada.

Esmeralda County—Goldfield

Early residents at times lamented the lack of a library in Goldfield, the town famous in 1902 for its fabulously rich "jewelry ore." Although it received much national notoriety for its wealth, its labor disputes, and its prizefights, it did not prosper long enough to establish a place for its readers. At one point Andrew Carnegie himself considered giving the community $20,000 if it could meet his requirements for matching funds,[24] but they were never fulfilled. The once-famous bonanza town began to decline in 1910, fell on hard times before the 1920s, and has not revived since. It survives primarily as one of Nevada's most impoverished county seats.

The community received bookmobile service from Clark County beginning in 1974. For a few years thereafter, some books were made available from that source and distributed from a room in the courthouse. When Jean Ford visited the library in the early 1980s she learned the Esmeralda County commissioners were providing $70 per month to a woman who opened the collection for clients four hours each week. Matters improved considerably in later years. Esmeralda County also supports small libraries in Fish Lake Valley and Silver Peak.

Storey County—Virginia City

The oldest and most famous of Nevada's mining camps, perched
on the slopes of Mount Davidson, was one of the last to establish
its own public library. Having dwindled from its prosperous 1870s
bonanza days to a tiny town of about seven hundred residents relying on tourism in the 1970s, it had been dependent for decades on
library services provided from Reno or Carson City or occasional
bookmobile visits from Fallon.

Finally in 1985, when it appeared that lending privileges offered
by Washoe County might no longer be available, the Storey County
commissioners appointed a library board, which decided to join
with the county school district in promoting a bond issue that
would build not only a new school but also a library for the entire
community. Voters approved the bond issue, and the library went
into service in 1986. The Churchill County Library donated four
thousand books previously assigned to its bookmobile collection.

A RETROSPECTIVE

Having taken a descriptive tour of the local libraries of the Sagebrush State, let us pause momentarily and catch our breath, before
we move on to Clark County, to reflect on the changes that have
occurred in the past hundred years for the book lover and information seeker.

For those of us who were nourished on the cozy, crowded one-
room book chambers such as those that still operated in Tonopah
and Pioche in 2000, the revolution that has occurred is dazzling. It
is no less sensational than the revolutions that have brought us jet
airlines, superhighways crowded with petroleum-fueled motor
vehicles, computers, and the Internet.

It is worth remembering, at this juncture, that most often it was
women—grandmothers, mothers, teachers, friends of books and
children—who provided the energy and organizational skills to

create public libraries where none had existed previously. They provided the foundations on which more recent services have been built.

Even in small, remote rural libraries, patrons now have access to the panorama of learning and information made possible through the Internet. The introduction of CLAN (the Cooperative Libraries Automated Network), which ties together scores of rural institutions with the state library by means of the Internet, further reduced the isolation. Initiated in 1981 by the latter institution and the Carson City/Ormsby County and Churchill County Libraries, it was an "odd duck," in the words of Sally Edwards, but it proved to be the wave of the future. By the end of the century libraries in all rural counties stretching across central and southern Nevada were sharing their databases through this link. The state fire marshal, the Nevada Supreme Court Library, the U.S. Geological Survey, and Sierra Nevada College are also part of the network. This model of cooperation, developed in western Nevada, has been copied throughout the country.

Let us now approach the metropolitan dynamo called Las Vegas and chronicle the growth of its various library districts. Once again, it begins with the story of dedicated women laying the foundations before government help and technology were available.

CHAPTER SIX

Clark County

Founded as a railroad town in 1905 by Senator William A. Clark of Montana, Las Vegas did not have any collection worthy of the title "library" until more than ten years later. It made little progress for another three decades in giving substance to the name. Even after the construction of Hoover Dam on the Colorado River in the 1930s, the development of a vast industrial plant at Henderson (twelve miles distant) in 1941–1945, and the beginning of the gambling-tourism boom of the late 1940s, Las Vegas continued to be served by a library more appropriate for a small rural town than for a burgeoning city.

On Courthouse Square

Even though it was Nevada's second-largest city as early as 1930, Las Vegas had more trouble than its neighbors to the north in assembling the resources to serve a literary public. As usual, a women's group laid the foundations. The Mesquite Club, the most prestigious of the early cultural organizations, began collecting books in 1909 and petitioned the local government for a library as early as 1911, the same year a city charter was authorized and when Las Vegas had one thousand people. The library boosters inherited a small masonry building, erected in 1909 as the first Clark County courthouse. Ronald M. James, in his detailed history of Nevada courthouses, described it as an "unadorned, square and concrete building [which] included a Mission Revival parapet reminiscent of that used in the contemporaneous Esmeralda County courthouse in Goldfield. The simple courthouse symbolized a time when Las Vegas looked to Goldfield as the region's population and cultural center."[1]

The county officers occupied the space in 1909, but within five years it was too small for their needs. This was one of the earliest instances in Las Vegas of outgrowing a structure within a few months of the time it opened its doors. Because the courthouse had become redundant, it became available to the Mesquite Club, who brought in books and opened its library in 1916 with modest support from the city government. This was the only public book depository for the community until 1951, when the incorporated city had more than twenty-five thousand residents.

The women who managed the little collection relied heavily on gifts of books and sporadic voluntary fund-raising.[2] Mrs. Charles Sloan, librarian during the 1920s and 1930s, was able to add only about twelve volumes annually during the years of the Great Depression. Patrons seeking service knew her as a diligent guardian of books who threatened dire results if any precious volumes were kept out beyond the allotted time. She belonged to the era when librarians were regarded primarily as custodians of property and protectors of morals. Mrs. Sloan fits the profile offered by library historian Dee Garrison in her landmark monograph *Apostles of Culture*. Garrison contended that the feminization of the public libraries early in the century "did much to shape the inferior and precarious status of the public library as a cultural resource; it evolved into a kind of marginal kind of public amusement service."[3] Las Vegas was developing other, more flashy kinds of amusements during those years.

The Wartime Boom

Las Vegas historian Eugene P. Moehring has chronicled the dramatic transformation of Las Vegas as a result of the defense-related investments of the 1940s. "The war tried, tested, and transformed Las Vegas," he wrote. "The seemingly endless rounds of rationing, shortages, scrap drives and fund-raising measured the community's resolve. But, as it did for cities in California, New Mexico, Texas and other Sun Belt states, World War II both created and confirmed the strategic importance of Las Vegas, thereby enhancing its chances of attracting future defense programs. Fifteen years of frantic federal spending changed Las Vegas forever."[4]

Libraries, however, did not immediately benefit from the war-related expansion. Lacking any substantial government support until the 1950s, the small-city library lagged far behind other civic endeavors. Billie Mae Polson—a volunteer page at the local library in the 1940s, later a forty-year cataloger at UNLV, and twice-president of the NLA—remembered graphically a half-century later the cramped, uninviting quarters in the quaint old building on courthouse square.

In 1943, when the city's population stood at twelve thousand, Beda Brennecke Cornwall and her husband, attorney C. Norman Cornwall, arrived in Las Vegas and reacted to the library's predicament. Mrs. Cornwall became a pacesetter in a Citizens' Library Association that mobilized community leaders, including Al Cahlan, editor of the *Las Vegas Review Journal*. (Cahlan was, incidentally, a member of a prominent Reno family. He had used the Carnegie library in Reno and had graduated from the University of Nevada). The publicity and support from the professional community were important elements in subsequent fund-raising for the library. As Las Vegas's economy grew with wartime activities at Nellis Air Force Base and the building of a large magnesium plant at Henderson, the book-reading public expanded rapidly, but without the aid of a suitable public-book collection. After the war ended, the casino business became a magnet for even more investment and more people.

Las Vegas library boosters finally applied the organizing skills they had developed during the war, using door-to-door solicitations in 1949 and collecting $68,000 in donations over two or three years. They needed, however, $100,000. A major breakthrough came when the city commissioners provided a $30,000 grant to replace the old courthouse with a new building at Fourth Street and Mesquite Avenue, which opened its doors on June 1, 1952. Older civic groups joined the movement, and some casinos dedicated the winnings of one slot machine to the construction fund. Gretchen Schenk, in her 1958 report, called the Mesquite Avenue building a place "of outstanding utility and attractiveness."[5] Mrs. Cornwall continued to lead the Citizens' Library Association until 1972. The library structure inspired by her efforts served the city until 1990.

In the meantime, the concept of the public library was changing on the national level. As noted earlier, the Carnegie Foundation, the American Library Association, and the Social Science Research Council combined resources in the late 1940s to conduct the Public Library Inquiry, headed by Robert D. Leigh. He and his associates conceived of a new kind of library service, not only embracing entertainment and educational service to a literate public but also encouraging freedom of communication, expert guidance in study, social mediating forums for diverse constituencies, and advanced technological services.[6] Southern Nevada made many technical and social advances during the 1940s; Las Vegas was on its way to becoming the entertainment capital of America, but library development remained on the fringes of public concern for another two decades.

THE BEGINNINGS IN CLARK COUNTY

As late as 1965, when the population within the city limits of Las Vegas was approaching 100,000, the periphery of Clark County around the edges of the municipality had at least 80,000 additional residents who had no library of their own. Those whose homes were outside the municipal limits were required to pay a $5 fee and find a city taxpayer to vouch for them if they wanted to borrow books from the city library. By the late 1960s, the state library in Carson City had abandoned its effort to be a public lending library for the entire state.

Enter Jean Ford, who developed her skills for organizing people and getting political results in the trenches of library development in Clark County; early in her efforts she was dubbed the "new Beda Cornwall."[7] Beginning as a 35-year-old homemaker with no experience in government, she learned enough about the tax laws and the workings of government to assemble the rudimentary facts about Nevada politics: By passing petitions as Norcross and his allies had done in Reno six decades earlier, a group of citizens could establish a tax base specifically for library services in the unincorporated areas. Yet the statute under which the tax initiative could be placed on the ballot was hopelessly complicated for an area like suburban Clark County. Petitioners had to acquire the signatures of either half the property taxpayers or those owning at least half the property values in the district. This had been done easily in Reno sixty years earlier; it was monumental task in suburban Clark County in 1965.

Ford sought assistance from state librarian Mildred Heyer. She organized a team of sixty friends who circulated petitions in the unincorporated suburbs for several months, an arduous task that seemed likely to require years of effort. In January 1965, with a new legislative session beginning, Ford approached the Clark County delegation in Carson City to change the law to enable the petitioners to gather signatures of 10 percent of the taxpayers to put a library-tax proposal on the ballot—a grass roots effort *par excellence*. The typical opposition to any kind of new tax measure emerged, but the proposal finally prevailed. This time, the traditional inertia was less vocal than the coalition in favor of new libraries. Governor Grant Sawyer signed the bill into law in April 1965.[8]

"Anyway, the bill passed," Ford said later when she recorded her oral history. "This is an example of an absolute nobody, a little committee of people having a need, going to various people, getting help, getting information, following the system and making it happen. [laughter] I mean, it was incredible. I didn't realize all that significance until later."[9] She had learned a basic lesson about the empowerment of women through their determination to build a library. Later in her career she returned to this theme often as a politician and activist for social justice.

From that point onward, the energy quickened. Dedicated teams of book lovers began their petitions a second time with the new law as their vehicle. They placed the library-tax proposal on the ballot again and won the victory at the polls much as Norcross had done in Reno sixty-four years earlier, although the odds against them were much greater in this sprawling military-industrial-gambling metropolis. The county commissioners, unaccustomed to such grass roots efforts for libraries, formed a library district in October 1965 and appointed the first board two months later.[10]

Ford had begun with as little experience as the scores of other nurturing women who had preceded in library pioneering in northern and central Nevada a generation or two earlier. She did have the advantage of a good education to advance her cause, with the Fleischmann Foundation funding and federal support available. This combination of ingredients had not been available to the previous generation of dedicated women of rural northern Nevada. In the process of being liberated from a failed marriage, Ford was the right person at the right time to bring new energy to a flexible political environment.[11]

The original library in the unincorporated area of Clark County opened in 1966 in three rooms of an annex building at the Las Vegas airport. The familiar scenario followed, but in southern Nevada the pace was greatly accelerated. The collection expanded so rapidly that the little band of devotees fell behind in their chores. Within a year the book collection outgrew the space available and was moved to its second makeshift domicile—a shopping center on Tropicana Avenue near the university campus—which itself was only a decade old. The original library director, who assumed his duties on September 2, 1966, was Charles Atkins.

In March 1967, the county acquired the five-acre site at 1401 East Flamingo Road, the first permanent home for the rudimentary county library. The 1968 gift of $1.38 million from the Fleischmann Foundation enabled the board and staff to plan a 50,000-square-foot building with space for 220,000 volumes. Ground breaking occurred on January 17, 1969, and the library opened two years later. During the period of construction the library director was Hardin E. Smith.

While the library was being planned, the *Las Vegas Review Journal* printed an editorial reflecting the frustration of hundreds of citizens.

> For years the library facilities available to Las Vegas residents were not adequate to serve a good-sized high school. We have become aware of the fact that one of the first things some prospective residents examine is the library. One can often tell much about a community by its library. . . .
>
> We were very slow in recognizing the need for a library, but thanks to the efforts and dedication of a small group of concerned citizens the county is preparing to build a good facility.[12]

The building included not only the conventional resources but also a pioneering computer system, a small auditorium, a children's room, a painting collection prepared by the Las Vegas Artists' League, and resources for mailing books to clients in outlying areas. Near the end of construction, tedious disputes arose between the county and the contractors, detracting from the euphoria of the opening in January 1971, but they subsided after a few

months. "Walking into the new Clark County library is like walking into a playground for the mind," wrote a reporter for the *Las
Vegas Sun.*[13]

THE HUNSBERGER ERA, 1971–1992

During the next twenty years, the library systems of the county
and city evolved into one of the most dynamic in the nation under
the leadership of Charles Hunsberger, who became director of the
Clark County Library District in December 1971. An innovative
and hard-driving leader, he was equal to the challenges of building
a major library service network for the nation's fastest-growing
urban area. Among his innovations was the introduction of a computerized circulation system in cooperation with librarians at
UNLV, a project that arose from the poverty and opportunity of
both library-building institutions.

Progress came slowly at first because for the next decade the
county and city provided few tax dollars for new facilities; operating budgets came from the small property-tax assessment arranged
by Ford and her friends.[14] It required several years for Hunsberger
and other advocates to build the broad-based community support
necessary for truly generous funding. While fifty new schools were
built in Clark County in the 1970s, only one new public book depository was opened—the Charleston Heights Library and Arts
Center—with most financial backing from federal rather than local tax money. Library boosters organized a "Bucks for Books"
fund-raising campaign in 1982 and a chili cookoff in 1983 to supple-
ment the meager support from local tax sources.

Within the city limits, the original Las Vegas library took over
storefront space in the Charleston Plaza shopping center, and similar quarters were found for book outlets in Sunrise Manor and
West Las Vegas. The library board managed to provide modest
bookmobile service. All of these efforts were feeble in such a rap-

idly growing urban area. As late as 1980 the county public libraries had fewer than one book per capita in their collections.

Through the 1970s and 1980s Hunsberger managed to increase significantly the number of professional librarians on the staff, thereby expanding the range and competence of those serving the public. One innovation was opening special sections and expanding services for young people. He supervised the transition into the era of electronics, automation, and the computer, embracing the concept of the libraries as active information-service stations and centers for diverse cultural activities, in addition to being repository for tomes.

A significant ally in improving the libraries' stature was Clark "Danny" Lee, a businessman who joined the library board in 1982 and became its chairman the following year. Linking local commercial initiative with Hunsberger's daring, the board joined a movement to support a statewide bond issue submitted to the voters in the 1982 general election; it was narrowly defeated.

Two years later, with better planning, a $10 million bond proposal passed. Lee later became an effective lobbyist in Carson City at the legislature for library-related bills.

Early in Hunsberger's tenure, library boards and administrators of Las Vegas and Clark County explored possibilities for cooperating to offer better service to all residents of the metropolis. The city and county negotiated an agreement for shared management in the mid-1970s. Finally both groups agreed to a formal merger as the Las Vegas–Clark County Library District (LVCCLD). Formal consolidation was authorized during the 1985 legislative session, with leadership provided by state senator Joe Neal of North Las Vegas.

The $10 million statewide bond issue approved by the voters in 1984 allowed for an unprecedented transfusion of help to the Clark County libraries. The following year Clark County voters passed another bond issue, this time for $15 million, for the expansion of libraries, which meant that the LVCCLD could qualify for more than $7 million in state funding. These votes enabled the city and county to plan eight new facilities and to expand others during the next five years, including the Sunrise Library at 5400 Harris Avenue (1987), the Green Valley and Spring Valley Libraries (both opened in 1985 and expanded in 1988), the Rainbow Library (1986, 1989) on North Buffalo Drive, and the West Las Vegas Library on West Lake Mead Boulevard (1989), among others. In the more distant areas, libraries were either established or expanded in the late 1980s in Blue Diamond, Bunkerville, Indian Springs, Laughlin, Mesquite, Moapa Town and Moapa Valley, Mount Charleston, Overton, Sandy Valley, and Searchlight.[15]

As the outreach of the LVCCLD accelerated in the mid-1980s, the original Flamingo Road headquarters of the county library became overcrowded and required a major expansion project. The first renovation, begun in 1986, lasted several months. A second major expansion, in the early 1990s, required the transfer of much of the collection to another building. The renovated structure reopened in 1994 with enlarged space for books, staff, and patrons and with improved computer capabilities.

Since Hunsberger promoted the idea that libraries should be centers for the fine and performing arts as well as resources for those with literary interests, several complexes had galleries and centers for these purposes. In 1989 he received the Governor's Arts Council award for service to the arts. The LVCCLD won respect in Lincoln, Nye, and Esmeralda Counties as well as in rural parts of Clark County for outreach services. Assistant director Nancy Hudson helped implement the new telecommunications plan for the statewide computer network, which had been developed earlier by the state library.

As southern Nevada faced a scarcity of professional librarians, LVCCLD initiated a scholarship program to help southern Nevadans interested in library science attend training programs elsewhere and return to the district for employment.

As the twentieth anniversary of Hunsberger's appointment as

director approached in 1991, the community registered an affirmation of its newly found esteem for libraries: Voters approved an $80 million bond issue for more and enlarged facilities. This was the third and by far the largest authorization of local library-cultural centers in less than a decade. Once again Danny Lee, who by this time had departed from the board, was a resourceful organizer of the bond issue campaign.

This success was, ironically, the prelude to Hunsberger's downfall. Shortly after the passage of the 1991 bond issue, the *Review-Journal,* which had supported the bond issue, launched a journalistic attack against his policies for expanding library services to embrace the fine arts, on the grounds that such amenities were extravagant. For the next two years, the LVCCLD was embroiled in a bitter dispute over how and where the money should be spent and whether the policy of building libraries as cultural and artistic centers was appropriate. Personnel on the library board changed, and Hunsberger lost his base of support. He resigned under pressure in 1993.

The issues in this struggle were multifaceted. County commissioners raised questions about whether the library district had too much autonomy in the use of taxpayers' money; library patrons living on the west side contended that Hunsberger was insensitive in his remarks about African Americans and the library and cultural needs of their area.[16]

LVCCLD faced turmoil for several years after Hunsberger's departure. Part of the staff remained loyal to Hunsberger, and many resented the encroachment of the library board in matters regarded by professional librarians as their own domain. Darrell Batson, an effective director of extension programs for rural libraries in Clark County, replaced Hunsberger, but after a few years he became another victim of the strife. The board eventually hired a management firm, and the staff organized a labor union to represent their interests as tensions increased.

One of the stunning facilities that emerged near the end of the

Hunsberger era was the new Las Vegas library, opened in June 1990 near Cashman field; it received national attention for its striking architectural design.[17] The $13-million, 104,000-square-foot building included the Lied Children's Discovery Museum, designed to enhance the curiosity of young people. For many years this library was under the direction of Jack Gardner, a longtime professional librarian respected throughout the state.

The narrative of the evolution of the LVCCLD relates only part of the saga of library development in Clark County. Three other library districts evolved separately and continued to have their detached roles in 2000. Local pride and a sense of community independence runs deeply here, as in rural Nevada.

BOULDER CITY

The Boulder City Library, founded in 1933, had a more promising beginning than the Las Vegas Library because of support from U.S. Bureau of Reclamation commissioner Elwood Mead, who supervised construction of Boulder (Hoover) Dam. He persuaded the Library of Congress to lend the city three thousand volumes. The Six Companies, builders of the dam, paid the salary of a librarian, Ruth Wyman, who enlisted the assistance of local teachers in serving the schools and the public.

After the Six Companies had completed their work on the dam and left the community in 1936, the library was closed because no money was available to pay a librarian. Two years later, thirty Boulder City homemakers formed a committee to staff the library on a regular basis for several years. In 1942, the Bureau of Reclamation agreed to hire a full-time librarian, and supporters initiated a fund drive for supplies and equipment.

Late in 1943, Boulder City taxpayers petitioned for a tax of 10 cents for each $100 of valuation on their property assessments for library purposes, and the chamber of commerce launched a drive for funds to purchase new books. The original library was in an old municipal building that served until the early 1980s, although it had become badly overcrowded much earlier.

Boulder City received $850,000 from the Fleischmann Foundation, one of the last library grants from the foundation before it ceased operating. The new building was dedicated on January 23, 1982. For many years this facility was under the capable direction of Carol Gardner.[18] In recent years it has been headed by the highly respected Duncan McCoy.

HENDERSON DISTRICT PUBLIC LIBRARY

The first public library in Henderson opened in 1946, four years after the establishment of the town that lodged workers employed by the Basic Magnesium plant. It was located in a small room in the processing plant provided by the industrial company. Soon the magnesium manufacturer allowed the first librarian, Laura Johndal, to move the collection to a small house in the Basic (later Henderson) townsite.

Initial public money to operate the library came from the local school district. For two decades, from 1947 until 1967, Lydia Malcolm was librarian, and the small home (finally donated to the library) was enlarged four times between 1946 and 1983 to manage the growing collection and expanding services.[19]

Henderson finally got new quarters for its library in 1989 as a result of the state bond issue approved in 1984. It was named in honor of the late state senator James I. Gibson, who served in the legislature for more than twenty years. This facility was enlarged twice in the next decade; the population of Henderson and its environs expanded so rapidly that it was the second-largest urban center in the state, promising to surpass Reno soon after 2000.

Joan Kerschner resigned as state librarian and director of the Department of Museums, Library, and Arts to become director of the
Henderson library in 1999.

NORTH LAS VEGAS

The city of North Las Vegas has long been eager to build its own
cultural identity, distinct from that of its famous neighbor to the
south. Advocates of a library raised their voices as early as 1959 but
were not able to get results until October 1962, when they acquired temporary quarters in the chamber of commerce building.

When the city government designed a handsome civic center
in the early 1960s, a substantial library was part of the plan. In May
1963, with the population hovering around twenty-five thousand,
voters approved a large bond issue for improvements that included
a library set in a spacious fourteen-acre sward of grass, trees, and
plants.

Completed in December 1966 with fifteen thousand square
feet and space for thirty thousand books, this facility served residents of Paradise Valley and personnel of Nellis Air Force Base as
well as North Las Vegas. Like their counterparts in Henderson and
Boulder City, supporters in North Las Vegas avoided the tempta-
tion to merge with Las Vegas and Clark County when they consolidated in the 1980s, although some city leaders expressed a wish
to do so. In 1985 the city dedicated a large addition to the library,
including a community meeting room and other amenities. The
expansion had shelf space for eighty-five thousand volumes.

For its first thirty years, the library operated as a branch of the
North Las Vegas municipal government. In 1993 the city established a separate library district, although it continued to provide
administrative support and three of the five library board members
were also on the city council. In the mid-1990s the district was
given a 4.5-acre tract in northwest North Las Vegas for a second

library, planned eventually to become the main city library. The community also formed a Friends of the Library group to try to build the level of support that had been seen elsewhere.

CHAPTER SEVEN

The University of Nevada, Reno

The academic libraries of Nevada came into existence by much the same method as the public libraries, relying heavily on the service of volunteers and the generosity of donors. The libraries at the two universities and four community colleges were for considerable time on the fringes of the educational enterprises they were intended to serve. That situation was changing conspicuously at the end of the twentieth century, but in this sphere, as in many others, Nevada's institutions of higher learning had much catching up to do to overcome the period during which the state's publicly supported cultural institutions were impoverished.

Nevada's second-oldest library, yielding only to the state library in seniority, is at the University of Nevada in Reno. It can claim longevity dating back to 1887. Although it has been relocated on the campus four times, it has usually been crowded and malnourished, with fewer resources and less space than was needed to meet the basic requirements of the faculties and students. In 2001 it still was scattered across the campus and had a large part of its collection in storage, a result of its continuing struggle to provide the services expected of a land-grant university that embraces the arts and humanities as well as the sciences and professional fields.

When the University of Nevada opened the doors of Morrill Hall to thirty students and two faculty members in 1886, it had no library. The faculty operated for a decade with only a meager stock of books. Like the public libraries, faculty and student scholars depended heavily on gifts or loans of reading material. For the first fifteen years the title of "librarian" was held by Hannah K. Clapp, a conscientious educator who had been a pioneer in Carson City; initially she served as preceptress and had teaching duties as well. After becoming the full-time librarian in 1891 she, more than any other person, made the appeals and laid the foundations of the earliest accumulation of books and periodicals.[1] She had none of the professional training that Garrison's *Apostles of Culture* brought to the public library domain a century ago, but she was politically astute and as dedicated as her counterparts on the community level. She served as librarian of the university until her retirement in 1901.

In 1887 a small room (later called the Norcross Room) on the first floor of Morrill Hall was provided for the library. Although the collection grew slowly, the library had 5,819 books and 3,892 pamphlets by 1898, and regular purchases were being made. In that year the university refitted the basement of Morrill Hall to hold the collection, equip a reading room for students, and provide a working space for the librarian.[2]

President Joseph E. Stubbs, who led the tiny institution from 1894 to 1914, made regular appeals for better library budgets. He was realistic enough to know that the state legislature was not likely to grant what was needed. "I forbear asking for special consideration of the needs of the University library at this time," he wrote in 1900. "Members of the Board of Regents and the President of the University have made individual appeals to men of wealth to give a Library Building to the University. I still hope that the day is not far distant when some wise and generous man or woman of wealth will realize the supreme need of the University and supply it by the gift of a Library Building. The cost of a fine Library need not exceed twenty-five thousand dollars."[3]

Stubbs often repeated his hope that an unselfish philanthropist

would come to the rescue, but when it happened, Clarence and
Marie Louis Mackay bestowed their greatest largess on a school of
mines. It was a most welcome gift to be sure, but most of the library remained confined to the Morrill Hall basement, with some
specialized collections in other buildings or in a carpenter's shop.
Near the end of his tenure, Stubbs ventured the hope that the next
benefactor might give $250,000 for a handsome administration
building and library.

In 1913 the Board of Regents took up the plea for a new academic library, calling the existing space in Morrill for the book
collection "a disgrace to the Institution" and worrying about the
danger of fire. Saying that the university actually needed $50,000
for a decent building, the regents challenged the legislature to appropriate at least $10,000 for an adequate one.[4] And so it did.

The result was the small brick structure on the west side of the
quadrangle, first known as the Hall of English, later the journalism
building, and finally the Jones Visitor Center. It has served the university well for eighty-five years, but only briefly for the function
originally intended. It was deficient for library purposes from the
beginning and could not even hold the existing collection and the
three hundred students expected to use it when it opened in 1914.
"The little University Library building is too scant now to provide
for the books and pamphlets in its possession," President Walter E.
Clark wrote in 1920. "The reading-space . . . has been totally inadequate from the start."[5] A mezzanine floor added soon after the
original building was constructed provided some relief, but not
enough. Clark described the facility as a "makeshift." "An inadequate library cripples the work of all departments," he complained
in 1922.[6]

Fortunately the library had professional leadership by the time
it moved into the new quarters. Two short-term librarians had followed Clapp after her retirement, but in 1907 Joseph D. Layman,
who had spent nineteen years on the staff of the University of
California at Berkeley, took charge of the collection of 13,670 vol-

umes. During his tenure the number of volumes increased nearly fourfold, to more than fifty thousand, with only stop-gap quarters to accommodate them.

Finally in 1927 the long-awaited deliverance came, not from public funds but from a private donor. He was William A. Clark Jr. of Los Angeles. The benefactor (no relation of the university president) was the son of the millionaire mining magnate and rail-road builder from Montana. He wanted to bestow a major gift on the university in memory of his wife, Agnes McManus Clark, a native of Virginia City, and President Clark was quick to guide his gift to the university's most urgent need. Announced at the com-mencement ceremonies of 1926, the new building was completed in 1927.

For the first time in its fifty-three-year history (forty-one years in Reno), the little academy had a library edifice worthy of its as-pirations. Built and furnished at a cost of $250,000, the structure had three floors with stacks in the basement, offices and special-ized rooms at the ground level, and a spacious reading area and seminar rooms on the second floor. Clark furnished the main rooms in relative elegance with chairs, tables, and equipment of a quality previously unknown to the impoverished little academy. Meanwhile gifts of books, some of them of considerable value, continued to arrive from donors; each biennial report carried a list of these contributions. They, more than the dollars from taxpayers, gave the university the components of the collection in which it could take pride. When Layman retired at the end of the 1920s with the new library standing as a testimonial to his dedication and Clark's generosity, the university seemed to be poised for a happy future.

But then came the Great Depression and World War II. The university marked time during the economic downturn and lost enrollment during the early 1940s. The biennial reports of the li-brarian and presidents are testimonials to sacrifice and patience. Perusing the records for the twenty years following the opening of the Clark library, one looks in vain for signs that the library was becoming more equal to the university's hopes.

A librarian trained at the University of Wisconsin, Thea C. Thompson, became the director and chronicler from 1930 until 1944, the most frustrating time in a long history of adversity for the institution. She begged eloquently but mostly without result for help from the state. Over this period, the collection grew by only about eleven hundred volumes per year, and most of those were gifts. Faculty and students often complained that the books available were out of date. The university could not even afford to bind most of the periodicals it received. It struggled to keep abreast of processing the collection with the help of former librarian Joseph Layman, who returned voluntarily for many years after his retirement to assist the staff.

By 1944, near the end of Thompson's term, defects in the Clark building were evident. It lacked air conditioning; the high windows were difficult to open and close; acoustical problems were evident. Additionally, the basic maintenance of the collection had been necessarily delayed. Upon her retirement, Thompson reported that the library held 68,075 volumes, many of them uncataloged.

This was the situation inherited by James J. Hill, a quietly eloquent librarian from Oklahoma who directed the institution for the next seventeen years. He watched the collection grow to more than 150,000 and the student body increase from 472 to 2,555. A voice of conscience for the university on library matters, he had the satisfaction of participating in the move to the new Getchell Library in 1961.[7]

The library's burden increased in January 1945 when it became a depository for all publications of the U.S. government, which meant that it began to receive titles at the rate of fifteen thousand to twenty thousand annually. Hill worried frequently that he would lose his small staff because of the inadequate salaries he was able to offer them, and he provided eloquent testimony about the level of support a library should have according to the standards of

the American Library Association. His reports repeatedly emphasized the extent to which the growing collection was dependent
on gifts from the faculty and community.

Then came a break in the dreary chronicle. In 1950, for the first
time in more than twenty years, the patient director wrote an up-
beat report of the achievements of the previous biennium. Improved budgets accompanied the return of the veterans from
World War II, and Hill was able to purchase more books, increase
the budget for binding, improve lighting facilities, and install a
browsing room. "If the present financial support for the purchase
of books is maintained and proper funds for the binding of serials
is provided," he wrote, "we can hope to meet the minimum requirements of the American Library Association for the library of
a Class 1 University in about 16 years."[8]

Budgets for books and periodicals were comparatively better
during the 1950s, but as the resources grew, the strain on the staff
and the outmoded Clark building increased. In response to the
space problem, colleges and academic departments began to operate quasi-libraries of their own, with minimal control from Hill's
office.

Thereafter the fortunes of the libraries varied biennially. At
times budgets seemed ample, and occasionally a president would
find a small year-end surplus to enhance the library's funds. Hill
and his staff worked diligently to reduce the backlog of unbound
periodicals. The collection passed the 100,000-volume mark in
the 1952–1954 biennium. The faculties' wish list expanded
through the years; most of it went unfulfilled from biennium to
biennium, but Hill did much to raise the consciousness of the institution and the community.

One continuous bright ray on the horizon came from bequests,
many of them encouraged by a Friends of the University Library
group established in 1952 under the leadership of Robert Griffen,
a local businessman. This group added more than one thousand
volumes to the collection in the first five years.

In 1957, when the university was enduring the trauma associated with the authoritarian presidency of Minard W. Stout, an outside committee evaluating the university looked at the library in the context of its broader investigation.[9] The committee, headed by California political scientist Dean E. McHenry, recognized the library's long-standing deficiencies and anticipated the demand for building a collection of 300,000 volumes on the Reno campus during the 1960s, in view of the commitment to graduate studies and the standards of the American Library Association.

Recognizing the need for expanding the collection, the McHenry committee recommended that the task not be undertaken with undue haste. "There should be no hurried attempt to reach 300,000 volumes, say, by 1965 even given the space and stack capacity. Rather a program based on actual faculty and student need, growth, and usage is recommended."[10] The report recommended that the university cease distributing its collection across the campus in departmental units. The cautious approach of the McHenry team was wise but probably unnecessary, in view of the university's history and prospects.

In 1958 the traditional ten-year report of the Northwest Association of Schools and Colleges reaffirmed the library's predicament. "The present library is entirely inadequate for present needs and cannot be expanded as enrollment increases. The facilities are not satisfactory."[11]

The legislature finally addressed the problem in 1959 with an appropriation of more than $2.5 million for a new structure, to be located in the center of the campus. When construction began early in 1960, the collection stood at about 160,000 volumes, "bound and unbound, cataloged and otherwise." The regents voted to name the building for Nobel H. Getchell, a prominent northern Nevada mine owner and former state senator. In January 1962 the librarians, led by cataloger Sam Wood, organized a "book walk," during which volunteers would transport armloads of books from the Clark building to the Getchell. Hundreds of students, alumni, and friends appeared to help; they carried the books along the snow-covered street to their new, long-awaited home.

With open book stacks, spacious reading areas for students, seminar rooms, and faculty-study niches, the Getchell building symbolized a new dawn for the institution. The purchase of new volumes was accelerated, and several smaller sublibraries were absorbed into the main collection. The devoted director Hill stepped down in 1961 and was replaced by David W. Heron, formerly the assistant director of the Stanford University libraries.

To add to the euphoria, in 1964 the Fleischmann Foundation offered the university $200,000 for the purchase of books if it could raise $100,000 from private sources for the same purpose. The Friends of the University Library and the alumni association responded and helped raise the $100,000, giving the institution another boost in morale and resources. In addition, a special session of the state legislature, encouraged by Governor Sawyer, provided a supplementary book budget.

In the first few years after its opening, the Getchell Library building encouraged innovations that had been impossible a few years earlier. A dynamic policy of acquiring rare and unique material was initiated, new and larger collections of Nevada materials found a home there, and the university archives were systematized under the direction of Helen Poulton and Karen Gash. Joyce Ball brought new vigor to the public service and reference division. There was ample space for seminar rooms, graduate classes, and many other amenities previously unknown. The building provided temporary quarters for the collection of the National Judicial College. In 1977 the state appropriated funds for an addition on the north side of the Getchell building that doubled its size.

When Heron departed to accept a position at the University of Kansas, his successor in 1979 was Harold G. "Hap" Morehouse, who served as director (later called dean of libraries) for the next twenty-three years. Morehouse, having joined the staff in 1961, stepped down as dean in 1993, but he continued to work as a cataloger in 2002, holding one of the longest tenures in the history of Nevada librarianship. He remembers the 1960s as a golden age for the university library. During the next few years the legislature granted increased budgets for both books and staff.

Also during the Morehouse administration, UNR librarians worked closely with their colleagues at UNLV and in the community colleges to link all their libraries through compatible integrated computer systems. This has made it easier for faculty, students, and other patrons to use the online catalog to find and obtain books from all University and Community College System of Nevada UCCSN institutions. Under the leadership of systems librarian Carol Parkhurst, computerized systems were introduced to enhance circulation, serials, acquisitions, and cataloging systems.

By 1964, the university started offering doctoral degrees for the first time, prodding the library to build its research collections. Beginning in geology, chemistry, and physics, where the faculty resources were strongest, Ph.D. programs were gradually initiated in additional fields by the end of the decade, putting more pressures on the libraries to acquire specialized material. Branch libraries, established early when space problems were most acute, continued to grow at several locations: the agriculture library— later the life and health sciences library—in the Fleischmann agriculture building; the physical sciences library in the chemistry building; the mines and geology collection in the original Mackay building; the engineering library in the Scrugham engineering building; and later the Sol and Ella Savitt medical school library at the north end of the campus. In 2000, William and Myriam Pennington made a major gift to facilitate the construction of an enlarged medical library and classroom building.

The DeLaMare mines library, one of the favorite campus showpieces at the end of the century, was formed in 1997 by combining the former mines and engineering libraries within newly remodeled space in the Mackay School of Mines building. Named for

Grover W. "Dee" DeLaMare, a discoverer of rich gold deposits in northern Nevada, it was decorated and furnished in an attractive nineteenth-century style with gifts from private donors. It houses geology, engineering, and science collections as well as the printed resources on mining.

Although the libraries gradually improved as the years passed, their budgets were vulnerable to the occasional downturns in the state's economy and the belt-tightening that followed. Three times in the last three decades of the century the academic book-and-periodical budgets were slashed, maintenance and binding spending was deferred, and greater reliance was placed on classified staff and student assistants as the professional staff assumed extra duties. The number of professionally trained librarians did not increase nearly as rapidly as the enrollment or the advanced-degree offerings in the last quarter of the century. Often the faculties and professional staff had to make painful decisions about subscriptions to costly journals needed by specialized programs. In this pre-computer era, when decisions were made to suspend subscriptions, they were inevitably controversial.

When the faculty did its self-evaluation in preparation for the 1988 accreditation by the Northwest Association, they told the university that state financial support for the libraries would have to be increased if the institution were to become a major research institution in the Great Basin region. Using standards set by the Association of Research Libraries, the faculty said the university should be adding sixty-seven thousand volumes per year at a cost of $2 million to reach its goal, but the current budget allowed the purchase of only twenty-five thousand.[12]

Ten years later, the same message appeared in the self-evaluation: "Present funding levels for library and information services are inadequate and incompatible with the University's mission. This funding inadequacy has long been recognized but never adequately addressed. To their credit, the UNR libraries staff have been good stewards, innovatively using the funding which has been provided. Nevertheless ... UNR libraries has become or is becoming a bottleneck in UNR's pursuit of excellence due to the perennial under-funding."[13]

The era of electronic technology presented additional demands and opportunities in the 1990s. Fortunately the institution had the expertise of Steven D. Zink, dean of libraries and associate vice-president for information resources and technologies, who succeeded Morehouse in 1993. Zink and the professional staff accepted the new challenges with vigor. That the university performed as well as it did as an academic institution, approaching the level of a category 1 Carnegie research center, could be credited in no small measure to their work in support of the advanced research under way throughout the university. At the end of the century, the UNR libraries held about one million volumes, three million microforms, six thousand current periodical titles, and more than one hundred electronic databases. While this was still short of the kind of collection recommended for a university with UNR's range of programs, the collection marked substantial progress over the previous decade. The online databases, interlibrary loan and document-delivery services, and comprehensive government-publications depository reduced some of the handicaps caused by the limitations of the collection.[14] The seventy-thousand volume law library of the National Judicial College was also available on the Reno campus.

The university library has continued to benefit from the gifts of private donors. The friends of the library organization, established midcentury, set a goal in the late 1980s of building an endowment of $1 million for the benefit of the library; by 2000 it had raised or earned more than half that amount in cooperation with the University Foundation. In addition its members contributed frequently to special projects, e.g., to purchase rare items, to provide computer terminals, and to replace outmoded furniture. Mary Ansari, longtime assistant director, and her husband, Nazir, made it possible for the university to develop a valuable map collection. The Robert Zimmer Hawkins Foundation and hundreds of other donors have helped the library in numerous ways.

In 2001 the legislature appropriated approximately one-third of the $60 million needed for a new library complex at the north end of the campus, and planning and additional fund-raising were well under way.

CHAPTER EIGHT

The University of Nevada, Las Vegas

The tribulations of building an academic library in Las Vegas were not as prolonged as the ordeal of developing public libraries in Clark County, but they were no less arduous. While the groundwork of the future UNLV (previously known as Nevada Southern University) had been laid in the mid-1950s, students had to rely on the meager public or school collections, or on an assortment of volumes donated by local citizens or duplicates sent from the Reno campus.[1]

James Dickinson, the first faculty member assigned to Las Vegas from the parent institution upstate, built bookcases in space borrowed from the Las Vegas High School to accommodate the first books contributed to the southern branch. Celeste Lowe, who became legendary for her varied services to Nevada Southern (NSU), was the initial, *de facto* librarian before the collection could be organized. The first professional librarian, Mary Lee Bundy, joined the staff in 1956, the year before the first building—Maude Frazier Hall—opened with six thousand square feet available for the books and periodicals. Three years later, with the opening of Archie Grant Hall, the NSU library was transferred to slightly larger quarters.

Those in charge of the rudimentary collection for the first ten years—Alice Brown, Jerry Dye, Mary Fitzgerald, Billie Mae

Polson—were perpetually short of the basic resources needed by faculty and students. The Fleischmann Foundation, early in the period of its grants, acquired a five thousand volume private collection in Carson City in 1960 and sent it to Las Vegas. Other assorted gift volumes of greater or lesser value appeared before librarians had the means to process them. In addition to their normal duties, librarians were often summoned to help the administration with chores such as registration and record keeping.

Both the university and its book collection expanded rapidly but sporadically during the 1960s. As NSU achieved full autonomy and became UNLV, a more systematic policy of library development evolved under the direction of Harold H. J. Erickson. By 1965, at the end of its first decade, the library claimed about eighty thousand volumes; eight years later it had tripled its book inventory.

In the interim, fortunately, the university constructed the Dickinson Library, a circular one-story building including much glass to allow "maximum supervision by minimum staff," according to Alice Brown.[2] Opened in February 1963, it gave the staff adequate working space for the first time. It had to be expanded to three stories within the next few years, even as it was in use. "You don't think of jackhammers having a place in a library but we had to become accustomed to them," Brown wrote.[3] The second and third floors were completed early in 1967, having been used to store books even as construction proceeded. Because of its circular design and the amount of asbestos used in the original construction, the building could not readily be remodeled outward, creating acute pressures as the collections and usage grew in the 1970s.

UNLV awarded its first baccalaureate degrees in 1964. When the Northwest Association of Secondary and Higher Schools, the regional accrediting agency, evaluated the university library in the mid-1960s, however, it found the holdings to be inadequate for the four-year programs then being offered. The student population rose from less than four thousand in 1967 to nine thousand by

1980. Even as the professional libraries at UNLV struggled to de-
velop a collection worthy of their university, their services were
sought by the Las Vegas Public Library, the Nevada Memorial
Hospital, the Atomic Energy Commission, the Environmental
Protection Agency, and other institutions.[4] The professional staff
worked valiantly to meet the requests from other agencies, public
schools, and patrons from the community. In 1968 they had to
cease their lending privileges to the general public because of the
growing needs of the university's scholars.

The UNLV librarians became allies of Jean Ford in her efforts to
pass petitions to create a library district for Clark County with its
own dependable tax base. The opening of the new public library
on East Flamingo Road a few blocks from the campus temporarily
eased the pressures on the Dickinson building.

In 1981, the four-story rectangular building arose north of the
Dickinson Library, and the two structures were connected by a
corridor at the second floor level. Because of fire codes it was not
attached to the original circular structure, so a tubular walkway
was built to connect the two units at the second- and third-floor
levels. This was an awkward solution that placed the book stacks in
one structure and most administrative and service units in the
other.

Polson, who worked at the NSU-UNLV library for forty years as a
cataloger and director of technical services, epitomized the dedication and good cheer that the handful of professional librarians
brought to their task as their responsibilities grew. As Las Vegas established its reputation as an international entertainment center
and home of nuclear-energy experimentation, the demands on
the staff were enormous. The politics of the dynamic community
and the university swirled around them while they tried to adapt
to the computer revolution and the demographic explosion simultaneously.

During the 1970s, Robert Anderl and Tom Kendall introduced
the emerging electronic technology to simplify the locating and

borrowing of periodicals, setting an example that was followed in other libraries throughout the state. By the 1980s the staff was building databases to connect the institution with its sister institution in Reno and with the Internet. UNLV was a leader in this field, prompted by the late beginning Las Vegas had made in conventional library development.

By 1990, when UNLV had five hundred faculty and enrolled more than sixteen thousand students, its library was still providing extensive service to the community at large; adult patrons from throughout the Las Vegas Valley were allowed to borrow books, and nearly one-third of the lending was to these nonacademic clients.[5] This was a generous gesture for an institution struggling to serve 120 undergraduate, masters, and doctoral-degree programs and to build research collections as well.

The Dickinson Library still fell far short of the of the standards for an institution of the size of UNLV, according to Dean of Libraries Mary Dale Deacon. She wrote in December 1989: "Annual increases in enrollment, the shift in institutional emphasis from undergraduate to professional and graduate programs and the extraordinary rise in the rate of inflation for library material beginning in the mid-1970's all have had a devastating impact on the library's ability to provide appropriate collection resources. While the library now supports all undergraduate programs, its collection is insufficient in both depth and scope to support graduate and professional research."[6] Using a formula based upon national standards, Deacon reported that the university should have had 715,000 volumes in its collection; instead it had 369,000, or 51.6 percent of the recommended number.[7]

In later years, the university addressed its library problems repeatedly, with prodding from faculty and students and the example of other academic institutions to guide it. Here, as in the realm of public libraries, its workers and friends built a foundation for a collection and a network worthy of a modern university.

On March 26, 1998, UNLV celebrated ground breaking for a totally new five-story, 300,000-square-foot library complex in the center of the campus. This facility was financed in part with funds from the Lied Foundation and other gifts and with additional appropriations from the state legislature. Opened in January 2001, it has seating capacity for twenty-five hundred readers and features an Automatic Storage and Retrieval System (ASRS), which enables patrons to have books on the stacks selected and delivered by electronic robots. The most current resources in computer catalogs and work stations became available in an "information commons."

At the end of the twentieth century the UNLV libraries contained 800,000 monographs, approximately 7,500 serials subscriptions, more than 90,000 nonbook materials such as video and music compact discs, and 1.5 million items in microforms. There are also ancillary collections in the College of Education and in the architectural-studies division.[8] The special-collections division has a gaming-research division that is one of the best of its kind. With the opening of new professional schools in architecture and law, the needs of the library users expanded sharply, but in these instances the resources were infinitely richer than they had been only a generation earlier.

CHAPTER NINE

The Community Colleges

While the universities struggled to build research collections to serve the diverse literary, scientific, and technical needs of faculties and students, Nevada's four community colleges began to assemble traditional libraries by the same tedious process that the public libraries had known. They solicited and accepted donations of books and used any niches and crannies they could find to store them.

Coincidental with the first years of these libraries, the computer-electronic revolution arrived. They built "learning centers" rather than libraries in the beginning. This resulted from low budgets and from the technological revolution.

Founded in the late 1960s (in Elko) or in 1971 (in Carson City, Reno, and Las Vegas), the colleges were latecomers to the field of library development. Book budgets were meager at best, and the part-time students who were the main clients often wanted technical training in the electronic fields rather than traditional book learning. Up-to-date collections in these areas were so costly they could not be built quickly.

At the "learning centers," owning printed resource material was less important than having audio-visual devices or being "online." At the 1990 Governor's Conference on the Future of Libraries, a commentator summarized the prevailing attitude of the colleges:

"The primary purpose of the Learning Resource Centers is to support the college curriculum, therefore their collections mirror the courses offered."[1] All colleges emphasized resources in nursing, for example, because of the widespread interest in that field. The learning-resource professionals spoke of stocking the center with Web pages more often than building a printed collection. Thus they approached the library business from a different direction than did their country cousins. By the 1990s, the colleges were trying to blend the world of books with the computerized realms, as were the community libraries. Another revolution in library services was under way as the twentieth century ended.

GREAT BASIN COLLEGE

Elko's historic role in Nevada higher education has been greater than the size of the community. As the original home of the Nevada University Preparatory School in 1874 and the city where the state's first community college was established in 1967, Elko has identified itself as a civic pioneer for education in the Sagebrush State. It also had one of the earliest functioning high schools at the beginning of the twentieth century.

The Great Basin College (originally known as Elko Community College and later as Northern Nevada Community College) formed a learning resource center in 1969. The pioneer woman in this case was Elizabeth Sturm, who arrived with her husband, Pepper Sturm, when he was hired to teach political science. While Betsy, as she was affectionately called, did not have professional library training, she brought invaluable personal skills. She knew how to ask for useful books from the community, how to select them, and how to involve the embryonic faculty in making choices when dollars were available for purchases.

Charles Greenhaw, the foremost historian of the early years of the community-college movement in Nevada, wrote of her, "If you could win a black belt for building libraries, Betsy Sturm would have at least one and probably two."[2] When Sturm arrived, the college library consisted of about fifty volumes collected in the basement of a grammar school. She worked for most of the first year without pay, but within the next three years she laid the foundations of a respectable collection. The basic collection was funded by a $100,000 grant from the Fleischmann Foundation. She and Pepper were forced to leave in 1975 because they lacked the formal credentials required by a new administration, but she later worked at Western Nevada Community College and at Truckee Meadows Community College.

The director of the center in Elko since 1974 has been Juanita Karr, who supervised transition of the institution from a book-centered resource to one concentrating on the electronic media. Located from the early years in McMullen Hall, the facility was typically cramped by the growth in the 1990s. The 1997 legislature provided $2.5 million for a major expansion and the addition of several classrooms. From May 1998 until September 1999 the center was relocated off-campus in a downtown warehouse while construction proceeded. The rededication of the enlarged quarters in October 1999 was warmly welcomed by the college community at a convention of the Nevada Library Association.

As Great Basin College was authorized to offer upper-division courses in elementary education in 1999—the first stage in the transition to a four-year, baccalaureate-granting institution—the center was trying simultaneously to enhance its printed resources and to expand its electronic access.

WESTERN NEVADA COMMUNITY COLLEGE

The original Western Nevada Community College (WNCC) structure in Carson City, built in 1974 and named the Bristlecone Building, included space on the ground floor for a library. These

quarters, increasingly crowded as the faculty and student population grew, continued to serve for more than twenty-five years.
In 1999, the legislature appropriated $6.9 million for a separate
thirty-four-thousand-square-foot building that serves as both a student center and a library. The beginning of construction was sched-
uled for 2001.

WNCC offered classes at Fallon as early as 1971 to about 150 students, and a branch gradually evolved there through the next two
decades. This unit did not, however, have its own library until 1992,
when one was located in Stillwater Hall.[3] In 1997 WNCC received a
$400,000 gift from the estate of Alicia and Manuel Beck to im-
prove the library at the Fallon campus.[4] Mrs. Beck had attended
classes at the Fallon branch frequently during the 1980s.

Library and media services facilities have been developed at the
Douglas County campuses of WNCC as well. All library branches
are connected with other colleges and universities though the
Nevada Online Catalog (NEON).

TRUCKEE MEADOWS COMMUNITY COLLEGE

Betsy Sturm, founder of the college library at Elko, moved to
Reno in the mid-1970s and had responsibility for setting up the
learning center at WNCC in Carson City before the division between the north and south branches led to the emergence of a
separate institution—the Truckee Meadows Community College
in Reno—formally recognized in 1979. She became librarian under the presidency of James Eardley, when TMCC was just getting
started, and faced the challenge of starting yet another community
college library. Originally it was assumed that this branch did not
need a separate library because of its proximity to the UNR campus
and because its programs were largely vocational. Sturm was in-
strumental in scrapping that supposition.

Creative in stretching modest resources to their limit for nearly five years, she once again engaged the faculty in assembling the resources. The unit was organized to be "a library and more," acquiring audio-visual and data processing devices as well as books. By the time she retired in 1988, the institution was often referred to by her name. In the mid-1990s the Board of Regents officially designated the learning center the Elizabeth Sturm Library. One of her dedicated assistants was Martha W. Coon.

Located originally at the former Stead Air Force Base north of Reno (the first home of the north branch of WNCC), the first collection was jointly held by the college and a branch of the Washoe County library and housed in a former military mess hall. In 1976–1977 it was relocated to the Dandini campus on the hills north of Reno in the classroom facility later known as Red Mountain Building. It was moved three more times over the next twenty years, finally acquiring its own dedicated site overlooking the Truckee Meadows in 1996.

COMMUNITY COLLEGE OF SOUTHERN NEVADA

The fastest-growing unit in the University and Community College System of Nevada is Community College of Southern Nevada (CCSN). With more than thirty-three thousand students scattered across the burgeoning Las Vegas Valley and in a dozen other locations throughout the southern triangle, it has faced formidable challenges in providing its clients access to education materials.

For many years the central information units on the three main campuses—in North Las Vegas (Cheyenne campus), at Henderson, and on West Charleston Street—were called learning resource centers because there was much emphasis on computers and other forms of visual aid to assist in the varieties of vocational and technical training the college featured. By 1990, however, CCSN had accumulated forty thousand books at the three campuses.[5] In the mid-1990s the term *library* became more commonly used as the book collections grew and as budgets became more nearly adequate.

Rose Ellis, director of the libraries in the late 1990s, noted a distinct improvement in the literary skills and educational interest of the student clientele near the end of the decade. Each campus not only has built a core collection of printed material in the arts and sciences but also has greatly enhanced the services offered on the Web.

CONCLUSION

Although Nevada's library systems have made tangible progress in bringing their services to urban and suburban neighborhoods and remote corners, rural areas and academic constituencies, the state's record at the end of the twentieth century was still mediocre when compared with most others. In 1990, the total operating expenditures per capita for public libraries nationwide was $16.28; in Nevada the figure was $9.84.[6] In evaluating the size of library holdings the facts were likewise bleak. The national average of the states showed 2.53 units per capita in public libraries, while in Nevada the figure was 1.51.[7] The Las Vegas area's status as the fastest-growing metropolitan region in the country partly explains this phenomenon. Despite the remarkable expansion of the library districts, the population increase was even larger. The statistics for 1995 showed that Nevada was still lagging at least 10 percent behind the national average in per capita spending for library operations.[8]

The most important revolution of the last half the twentieth century was the information revolution; this has been so often asserted that it has become a cliché. It is a marvel especially dazzling to those of us who began using libraries more than fifty years ago, when our small-town collections were precious little caches of dusty volumes gathered by dedicated mothers and spinsters. But it is worth remembering that about a hundred years ago an earlier version of the information revolution was occurring, with the initiation of the public libraries and the establishment of the first academic library in Nevada.

At the beginning of the twentieth century, the free public library movement was in its infancy. The idea that every community of modest size could and should have a library was a logical extension of the ideal of Jeffersonian democracy. Its implementation was encouraged by the bequests of Andrew Carnegie and by the political initiative of book lovers like Frank Norcross and Jean Ford. But just as important to the fulfilling of the embryonic dream was the energy and dedication of those who gathered the reading material, donated and begged for the initial money and volumes, and mobilized the ill-defined curiosity into political action.

As the twenty-first century opened, information was literally at our fingertips. We can call up from our computers in a few moments what previous generations worked tediously to acquire and catalog in hard copies. In the distant past, the lifetime labor of priests and monks founded the first libraries in the Western world; more recently in America it was usually dedicated, unpaid or underpaid women volunteers who provided the inspiration and built the data bases. We bookish and/or "computer-literate" patrons will be forever in the debt of those who laid the foundations for the contemporary libraries.

We have a challenge much different at the beginning of the twenty-first century from the one that confronted our forebears a hundred years ago. Their problem was a poverty of information; ours is a glut. Curious minds were hungry for fruitful ideas a hundred years ago; now we have an avalanche of trash.

What is the library's obligation in this era? This has been a topic widely discussed among librarians. Early in the twentieth century it was thought to be to give the clients carefully screened, wholesome educational and entertaining material. The librarians of my youthful reading years would not have tolerated "trash" in the sanctuary where I found food for the mind—"trash" in those days meaning erotically suggestive reading matter or ideas that were politically offensive. Far more insidious are those sirens that would lead us from the engagement with books to the psychedelic attractions of our time.

James H. Billington's ideas about the role of the public library, mentioned in the introduction to this book, are worth further discussion.[9] The library cannot and should not edit or restrain the trash, but it has a profound obligation to offer alternatives.

For book lovers and computer addicts alike, building a good library is an exhilarating, even exotic, experience. Whether we assemble our personal collections from pennies saved or help create an institution to inform and empower future generations, we can be thrilled by the process. So it was on the Western frontier wanting in reading matter, and so it is in the age of electronic retrieval. In the olden days not so long ago, we "surfed the net" in the volumes available to us in the comfort of a cozy room at home, at school, or in the questionable comfort of the nearest town library. So may it be in the new millennium with the new tools and toys.

Notes

INTRODUCTION

1. Russell R. Elliott, *Nevada's Twentieth-Century Mining Boom: Tonopah, Goldfield, Ely* (Reno: University of Nevada Press, 1966).

2. The standard work in this field is Anne Bail Howard, *The Long Campaign: A Biography of Anne Martin* (Reno: University of Nevada Press, 1985). See also the excellent contribution of Anita Ernst Watson, *Into Their Own: Nevada Women Emerging into Public Life* (Reno: Nevada Humanities Committee, 2000).

3. Dee Garrison, *Apostles of Culture: The Public Librarian and American Society, 1876–1920* (New York: Free Press, 1979).

4. Joanne E. Passet, *Cultural Crusaders: Women Librarians in the American West, 1900–1917* (Albuquerque: University of New Mexico Press, 1994).

5. Karen J. Blair, *The Clubwoman as Feminist: True Womanhood Redefined, 1868–1914* (New York: Holmes & Meier, 1980), 99–100.

6. Lowell A. Martin, *Enrichment: A History of the Public Library in the United States in the Twentieth Century* (Lanham, Md.: Scarecrow Press, 1998), 17.

7. Nevada Department of Museums, Library, and Arts, *Nevada Library Directory and Statistics: 2001* (Carson City, 2001), 1–8.

8. James H. Billington, "American Public Libraries in the Information Age: Constant Purpose in Changing Times," *Libraries and Culture* 33, no. 1 (winter 1988): 12.

9. Jean Ford, *A Nevada Woman Shows the Way* (Reno: University of Nevada Oral History Program, 1998). The book is based on oral interviews conducted and edited by Victoria Ford.

CHAPTER ONE. THE FIRST FORTY YEARS

1. *Gold Hill News,* November 11, 1865, 2–1. *Territorial Enterprise* (Virginia City), March 31, 1867, p. 3, col. 1; June 21, 1870, p. 3, col. 1. An 1875 report on public libraries issued by the Department of the Interior reported that the International Order of Odd Fellows library had thirty-three hundred volumes and the Masonic library had twenty-one hundred (U.S. Department of the Interior, *Public Libraries* [1875]).

2. In 1959, Martha Breen, a student at the University of Nevada in Reno under the direction of Professor Charlton Laird, wrote "A Brief History of the Miners' Union Library Collection of Virginia City, Nevada," which exists in the Special Collections Department of the UNR library. Some of these books made their way to a "Museum of Memories" in Virginia City in the 1930s and were eventually acquired by the University of Nevada in 1937. At least two hundred of these volumes remained in the UNR library Special Collections Department in 1999. See also *Sagebrush,* November 17, 1939, and [Myron Angel], ed., *Thompson and West's* History of Nevada (1881; Berkeley: Howell-North, 1958), 261.

3. Martin, *Enrichment,* 2.

4. *Report of the Secretary of the Interior* (Washington, D.C.: Government Printing Office, 1894), 3:713, 717.

5. Russell R. Elliott, *History of Nevada* (Lincoln: University of Nebraska Press, 1973), 375.

6. *Statutes of the State of Nevada* (1895), chap. 90, pp. 79–81.

7. Ibid. (1897), chap. 26, p. 30.

8. The correspondence between Norcross and Carnegie was published in the *Nevada State Journal,* March 29, 1902, p. 1, cols. 3–5.

9. Ibid., May 22, 1902, 5:3.

10. Theodore Jones, *Carnegie Libraries across America: A Public Legacy* (New York: John Wiley & Sons, 1997), 2–3.

11. Abigail A. Van Slyk, *Free to All: Carnegie Libraries and American Culture, 1890–1920* (Chicago: University of Chicago Press, 1995), 133.

12. "The Carnegie Library," *Reno Evening Gazette,* June 4, 1904.

13. When Norcross prepared autobiographical statements in later years, he regularly mentioned his work on behalf of the free public library in Reno. See, for example, his biography in Sam P. Davis, ed., *The History of Nevada* (Reno: Elms Publishing Co., 1913), 2:1067–69.

CHAPTER TWO. THE STATE LIBRARY:
THE FIRST CENTURY, 1865–1965

1. *Laws of the Territory of Nevada* (1861), chap. 89, p. 295. In the *Annual Reports of the Territorial Auditor, Treasurer, Superintendent of Public Instruction, and Adjutant General* (Carson City: Territorial Printer, 1864), 5, the territorial auditor wrote, "During the past year I have had a room fitted with shelves in the rear of my office, and the books removed thereto. There are about six hundred and fifty volumes, mostly Congressional and State Documents, in the library. Congress at its last Session made an appropriation of twenty-five hundred dollars for the purchase of books, but the money has never been received."

2. *Statutes of the State of Nevada* (1864–65), chap. 43, pp. 153–54.

3. Ibid., chap. 143, pp. 409–11.

4. Ibid. (1875), chap. 94, p. 150.

5. Department of the Interior, Bureau of Education, *Public Libraries in the United States of America . . . Special Report,* pt. 1 (1876), 791.

6. *Statutes of the State of Nevada* (1877), chap. 97, p. 166; Assembly Concurrent Resolution No. 4, ibid., p. 213.

7. Ibid. (1883), chap. 75, p. 101.

8. Nevada State Library, "Report of the State Librarian for the Years 1887–1888," in *Appendix to the Journal of the Senate and Assembly* (1889), 4.

9. Nevada State Library, "Report of Librarian" (1893), in *Appendix to the Journal of the Senate and Assembly.*

10. "Report of the State Librarian," in "Biennial Report of the Secretary of State," *Appendix to the Journal of the Senate and Assembly* (1899), 86.

11. *Statutes of the State of Nevada* (1905), chap. 87, pp. 188–90.

12. *Biennial Report of the Superintendent of Public Instruction, 1903–1904* (Carson City: State Printing Office, 1905), 15.

13. "Report of State Librarian," in "Report of the Secretary of State," *Appendix to the Journal of the Senate and Assembly* (1913), 204.

14. "Biennial Report of the Secretary of State and Ex Officio State Librarian," in *Appendix to the Journal of the Senate and Assembly, 1913–1914* (1915), 64–65.

15. *Statutes of the State of Nevada* (1915), chap. 202, pp. 310–11.

16. Ibid. (1917), chap. 185, pp. 347–48.

17. *Biennial Report of the State Library Commission* (1934).

18. Marriage's first report is the eleventh *Biennial Report of the State Library Commission* (1936).

19. *Biennial Report of the State Library Commission,* July 1, 1938–June 30, 1940 (1940), 7.

20. The figures from the Washoe County Library and the Nevada State Library include the volumes in the law libraries.

21. "Report of the State Librarian," in *Appendix to the Journal of the Senate and Assembly* (1946), 7.

22. Edwin Castagna, in "Books and Libraries in the Sweet Promised Land of Nevada" (an address to Nevada Library Association in Reno, October 13, 1959), 7, identified these six as himself, Marco Thorne, James J. Hill, Charles Marriage, Cornelia Provines, and Arlene DeRuff.

23. *Nevada Librarian* (mimeographed newsletter of the Nevada Library Association) 1, no. 1 (July 5, 1946).

24. Ibid., 1, no. 3 (November 3, 1946).

25. *Statutes of the State of Nevada* (1949), chap. 276, pp. 576–79.

26. Edwin Castagna, "Censorship, Intellectual Freedom, and Libraries," in *Advances in Librarianship* (New York: Academic Press, 1971), 2:215–51.

27. Robert D. Leigh, *The Public Library in the United States* (New York: Columbia University Press, 1950).

28. Ibid., 25.

29. Ibid., 245.

30. Helpful insights are to be found in Deanna LaBonge, "Women in Northern Nevada Libraries: Past and Present" (article for a course directed by Jean Ford at UNR, [1997?]), copy of typescript in Jean Ford's papers, in the Nevada State Library.

31. An excellent collection of essays can be found in Suzanne Hildenbrand, ed., *Reclaiming the American Library Past: Writing the Women In* (Norwood, N.J.: Ablex Publishing Co., 1996).

32. Assembly Resolution 29, *Journal of the Assembly* (1953), 274–75.

33. Nevada Legislative Council Bureau, *Legislation Toward Effective Library and Related Services for the People of Nevada,* Bulletin no. 25 (December 1954).

34. Ibid., 3.

35. Gretchen Knief Schenk, "Public Library Service in Nevada" (1958), in *Appendix to the Journal of the Senate and Assembly* (1959).

36. Ibid., 9.

37. Ibid., 13.

38. Ibid., 15.

39. Ibid., 36–39.

40. Ibid., 59–63.

41. *Statutes of the State of Nevada* (1959), chaps. 234, 235, 260, pp. 279–80, 328.

42. *Congressional Record,* 84th Cong., 2d sess., 1956, 102, pt. 6:7696–97.

CHAPTER THREE. SINCE 1965: THE STATE LIBRARY, THE NEVADA LIBRARY ASSOCIATION, AND FLEISCHMANN GIFTS

1. "First Report: Nevada Libraries—1966," *Nevada Council on Libraries* (January 1967): 9.

2. *Nevada State Library—Report* (July 1964–June 1966), 9.

3. *Reno Evening Gazette,* December 18, 1964, 20.

4. *Statutes of the State of Nevada* (1965), chap. 186, pp. 331–33.

5. Ibid.

6. Ibid., chap. 236, p. 430.

7. As the Fleischmann Foundation was terminating its work in 1980 according to Major Fleischmann's wishes (twenty years after the death of his wife), it published a small report entitled *Max C. Fleischmann Foundation: Twenty-Eight Years. A Narrative Report of the Foundation's Activities.*

8. *Statutes of the State of Nevada* (1983), chap. 328, pp. 801–2.

9. *Dateline: State Library* (January–February–March 1986): 2–4.

10. Guy Shipler, "Nevada's Libraries Malnourished," *Nevada State Record* (April 9, 1985), 2.

11. *Statutes of the State of Nevada* (1993), chap. 466, pp. 1579 ff.

12. *InfoConnection: Nevada State Library and Archives* 2, no. 4 (October–December 1992): 7.

13. *Statutes of the State of Nevada* (1963), chap. 153, pp. 219–20.

14. A useful, seven-page summary of the first thirty-five years, "History of the Nevada Library Association," was adapted by Bille Mae Polson of the UNLV library in 1980 from *Encylopedia of Library and Information Science* (New York: Marcel Dekker, 1976), 19:307–16. Polson's revision is available in typescript in the files of NLA.

CHAPTER FOUR. WASHOE COUNTY

1. A series of historical articles appeared in the *Nevada State Journal* in 1948 written by John Hamlin (August 15, p. 16; August 22, p. 12; August 29, p. 14; September 5, p. 16; September 12, p. 15; September 19, p. 13; September 26, p. 14) and by Edwin Castagna (October 3, p. 10; October 10, p. 13; October 17, p. 16).

2. Howard, *Long Campaign,* 17–31.

3. *Reno Evening Gazette,* December 7, 1887, p. 3, col. 2; December 13, 1887, p. 3, col. 3.

4. *Nevada State Journal,* January 23, 1901, p. 3, col. 4; February 2, 1901, p. 3, col. 4.

5. *Statutes of the State of Nevada* (1901), chap. 96, p. 99.

6. *Statutes of the State of Nevada* (1903), chap. 22, pp. 42–43. For a general summary, see the article by Dick Rhyno, "Brief History of the Washoe County Library System," *High Roller* 20, no. 2 (1983): 25.

7. "Free Library Is Now Open," *Reno Evening Gazette,* May 31, 1904.

8. "Secretary's Report," in *First Biennial Report of the Nevada Historical Society—1907–1908* (Carson City: State Printing Office, 1909), 19.

9. *Nevada State Journal,* February 1, 1941, 7.

10. *Reno Evening Gazette,* January 11, 1930. The laws are in *Statutes of the State of Nevada* (1929), chap. 140, p. 179, and chap. 168, pp. 268–72.

11. Schenk, *Public Library Service,* 12.

12. *Reno Evening Gazette,* January 22, 1966, 9.

13. *Reno Gazette-Journal,* July 15, 1979, sec. B, p. 10.

14. Don Vetter, "How Washoe Library Lost Its Hunt for Funds," *Reno Gazette-Journal,* March 31, 1986, sec. A, pp. 1 ff.

15. *Final Report of the Citizens' Blue Ribbon Advisory Committee on the Future of Washoe County Library,* February 1987.

16. An explanation of this adjustment can be found in Michael J. Bowers, *The Sagebrush State: Nevada's History, Government, and Politics* (Reno: University of Nevada Press, 1996), 117.

17. *Reno Evening Gazette,* January 25, 1905, 8:4. This collection had originated in Wadsworth, the predecessor of Sparks as the division point, and was moved to Sparks in 1904–1905.

18. *Reno Evening Gazette,* July 8, 1908, 8:1–2.

19. *Statutes of the State of Nevada* (1931), chap. 42, pp. 49–51. Madeline Mendive, "Sparks Library," *Reno Evening Gazette,* May 22, 1958, 3.

20. *Sparks Tribune,* April 9, 1980.

21. *Reno Evening Gazette,* February 8, 1984, sec. C, p. 1.

CHAPTER FIVE. FIFTEEN COUNTIES: A PANORAMA

1. Passet, *Cultural Crusaders,* 90, 177.

2. Ibid., 7 ff.

3. Watson, *Into Their Own,* 23–31.

4. The basic information on Tonopah's library was assembled in 1966 by Helen Hood, the clerk of the Tonopah Library Board. It was made available to Linda P. Newman for her "Early Public Libraries of Nevada" (typescript in Special Collections Department, Getchell Library, University of Nevada, Reno) and has been reprinted frequently since. Additional material is available in Robert D. McCracken, *A History of Tonopah, Nevada* (Tonopah: Nye County Press, 1992), 55–57.

5. Mrs. Hugh Brown, *Lady in Boomtown: Miners and Manners on the Nevada Frontier* (Reno: University of Nevada Press, 1991).

6. This information was provided by Diane Hartsock in an interview on August 4, 1999, at the Tonopah Library.

7. "Dorothy Shirkey Community Library," in *High Roller* 20, no. 2 (1983): 28–30.

8. Ruth Fenstermaker Danner, *Gabbs Valley, Nevada: Its History and Legend* (Winnemucca: Ruth Danner, 1992), 286–88.

9. *White Pine News,* March 12, 1916.

10. Ibid., July 2, 1916.

11. Ibid., April 1, 1917.

12. Bob Gray, "White Pine County Library," *High Roller* 20, no. 2 (1983): 39.

13. Hailie T. Gunn, Elko county librarian after 1969, wrote a brief history, which was printed in the *Elko Daily Free Press,* April 7, 1984, 9.

14. The history of the Humboldt County libraries has been prepared by J. P. Marden, "Early Winnemucca Libraries," available in typescript at the Humboldt County Library.

15. *Silver State,* February 8, 1923, 1:7. Marden, "Early Winnemucca Libraries," 3–4.

16. *Statutes of the State of Nevada,* 1925, chap. 189, pp. 331–32.

17. This information was provided by Jeanne Munk, who has been on the Pershing County Library staff since 1980 and director since 1990. See the *Lovelock Review-Miner,* June 20, 1930, p. 1, col. 4.

18. Barbara Mathews and Dora Witt, "Churchill County Library: A Place for the Reader," *Churchill County: In Focus,* annual journal of the Churchill County Museum Association (Fallon: 1987–88): 36–39. Mathews has been helpful in providing additional information. Sharon Lee Taylor wrote an extensive article in 1985 in a newsprint publication called "Hidden Treasures of Churchill County," issued April 20, 1985.

19. *High Roller* 20, no. 2 (1983).

20. Material on the Pioche library was gathered in 1969 by Mrs. Pearl Sorensen, then the Lincoln County librarian. Her typescript was placed in the Field Services Division of the Nevada State Library. See Newman, "Early Public Libraries of Nevada," 24–25.

21. The source for this information is Shannon Hammond, longtime Pioche librarian, and Joan Kerschner. See the *Lincoln County Record,* December 20, 1990. Peggy Draper, librarian of the late 1990s, provided much data on the history of the Pioche library.

22. Wynne M. Maule, *Minden, Nevada: The Story of a Unique Town, 1906–1992* (Minden: Wynne M. Maule, 1993), 51.

23. In the edition of the *Mineral County Independent* published on April 8, 1981, in honor of Hawthorne's centenary, a history of the local library appears, written by Lucy Colman and Bill Glenzer. This was reproduced in *High Roller* 20, no. 2 (1983).

24. *Goldfield Chronicle,* February 25, 1909.

CHAPTER SIX. CLARK COUNTY

1. Ronald M. James, *Temples of Justice: County Courthouses of Nevada,* foreword by Cliff Young (Reno: University of Nevada Press, 1994), 44.

2. An early history was written by Jean Ford and Sally Michaels for an article in the diamond jubilee issue of the *Las Vegas Sun,* June 16, 1980. An

expanded version, written by Dee Coakley and entitled "Our Libraries: How They Began," appeared in the *Las Vegas Sun Magazine,* March 27, 1983, 8–9, and April 3, 1983, 8–9.

3. Garrison, *Apostles of Culture,* 174.

4. Eugene P. Moehring, *Resort City in the Sunbelt: Las Vegas, 1930–1970* (Reno: University of Nevada Press, 1989), 40.

5. Schenk, *Public Library Service,* 11.

6. Leigh, *Public Library,* 6–11.

7. Ford described her efforts on behalf of libraries in *A Nevada Woman Shows the Way,* 87–93, 299–306.

8. *Statutes of Nevada* (1965), chap. 442, pp. 1216–18.

9. Ford, *A Nevada Woman,* 92.

10. Much of what follows is taken from a summary prepared by Ann Langevin in 1979.

11. Ford's oral history, *A Nevada Woman Leads the Way,* is worthy of much more than the ephemeral attention it receives in the present volume. It chronicles her persistent work for social justice and environmental responsibility as well as her crusading for the empowerment of women.

12. "Clark County Builds First Good Library," *Las Vegas Review Journal,* September 30, 1968.

13. *Las Vegas Sun,* January 17, 1971.

14. An excellent overview of the situation at the beginning of the 1980s appeared in the *Las Vegas Sun,* January 20, 1980, sec. E., p. 2.

15. Las Vegas–Clark County Library District, *The Decade of Expansion: 1979–1989 & 1990 Yearbook* (1990).

16. This controversy spawned an interesting thesis by John Thompson Stephens, "Political Control over Special Districts in Local Government: A Case Study of the Las Vegas–Clark County Library District" (master's thesis, UNLV, May 1996).

17. This building was featured in *American Libraries: The Journal of the American Library Association* 21, no. 10 (November 1990).

18. Dennis McBride, *In the Beginning . . . : A History of Boulder City, Nevada* 2d ed., rev. and enl. (Boulder City: Hoover Dam Museum, 1992), 49. Previously published by the *Las Vegas Sun.*

19. *High Roller* 20, no. 2 (fall 1983): 46.

CHAPTER SEVEN. THE UNIVERSITY OF NEVADA, RENO

1. Two individuals left typescript manuscripts of the early history of the UNR library; they are available in the Special Collections Department of the Getchell Library. The first is Clare L. Johnson, "History of the University of Nevada Library, 1876–1927," 7 pp. The second, more detailed, is James J. Hill, "A Short History of the University of Nevada Libraries," bringing the record to 1961. Hill's history was written to coincide with the seventy-fifth anniversary of the UNR library and the opening of the Getchell Library.

2. *Biennial Report of the Regents of the State University,* 1897–1898, 14–15.

3. Ibid., 1899–1900, 24.

4. *Biennial Report of the Regents of the University of Nevada,* 1911–1912, 9.

5. *Biennial Report of the Board of Regents,* 1919–1920, 46–47.

6. Ibid., 1921–1922, 20.

7. The typescript of his history in Special Collections contains the summaries from Hill's biennial reports.

8. *Report of the Regents of the University of Nevada,* 1948–1950, 74.

9. Nevada Legislative Counsel Buruea, *The University of Nevada: An Appraisal,* report of the university survey, Bulletin no. 28 (December 1956), 99–104.

10. Ibid., 104.

11. *University of Nevada Report to the Commission of the Northwest Association of Secondary and Higher Schools* (1958), typescript, 8–9.

12. University of Nevada, Reno, *Institutional Self-Study Report for the Commission on Colleges. Northwest Association of Schools and Colleges* (October 1988), vol. 2, Instructional Activities, 93–94.

13. Ibid. (October 1997), Standard IV, p. 64.

14. University of Nevada, Reno. *General Catalog, 1999–2000,* 15.

CHAPTER EIGHT. UNIVERSITY OF NEVADA, LAS VEGAS

1. For the early history of UNLV library see James W. Hulse, *The University of Nevada: A Centennial History* (Reno: University of Nevada Press, 1974), 202–3. A much more extensive account of the early struggles can be found in Alice Brown, "Memorable Moments: The First 25 Years of the

Library at the University of Nevada at Las Vegas," typescript, Special Collections Department, UNLV Library. Brown wrote the original narrative in the early 1980s and condensed it for *High Roller* 20, no. 2 (1983): 61.

2. Brown, "Memorable Moments," 8–9.

3. Ibid., 14.

4. Ibid., 10.

5. Mary Dale Deacon, "The James R. Dickinson Library," in Nevada State Library and Archives, *Libraries: Key to Democracy,* Governor's Conference on the Future of Libraries discussion papers, ed. Bonnie Buckley (February 1990), 11.

6. Ibid., 12.

7. Ibid., 13.

8. University of Nevada Las Vegas, *Undergraduate Catalog: 1998–2000,* 14.

CHAPTER NINE. THE COMMUNITY COLLEGES

1. Valerie Anderson, "Community College Library Resources in Nevada," in *Libraries: Key to Democracy,* 5.

2. Charles Greenhaw, "People's Colleges," Great Basin College, Elko, Nevada, is an extensive manuscript based on interviews with more than one hundred people who had shared the early years in the community college movement. It deserves the attention of anyone interested in education in Nevada. The Sturm interview is at pp. 185–88.

3. *Lahontan Valley News & Fallon Eagle Standard,* March 2, 1992, 2.

4. *Nevada Appeal,* January 15, 1997.

5. Anderson, "Community College Library Resources," 4.

6. U.S. Department of Education, Office of Educational Research and Improvement, *Public Libraries in the U.S.: 1990,* by E. D. Tabs (National Center for Education Statistics, June 1992), 92-028:42–43.

7. Ibid., 62, 64.

8. U.S. Department of Education, *Public Libraries in the United States: FY 1995,* by E. D. Tabs (National Center for Education Statistics, August 1998), 68. The average per capita expenditures for operations nationwide was $20.88; in Nevada it was $17.31.

9. Billington, "American Public Libraries."

Bibliography

PUBLISHED SOURCES
Books

[Angel, Myron], ed. *Thompson and West's* History of Nevada. 1881. Reprint, Berkeley: Howell-North, 1958.

Blair, Karen J. *The Clubwoman as Feminist: True Womanhood Redefined, 1868–1914.* New York: Holmes & Meier, 1980.

Bowers, Michael J. *The Sagebrush State: Nevada's History, Government, and Politics.* Reno: University of Nevada Press, 1996.

Brown, Mrs. Hugh. *Lady in Boomtown: Miners and Manners on the Nevada Frontier.* Reno: University of Nevada Press, 1991.

Danner, Ruth Fenstermaker. *Gabbs Valley, Nevada: Its History and Legend.* Winnemucca: Ruth Danner, 1992.

Davis, Sam P., ed. *The History of Nevada.* Reno: Elms Publishing Co., 1913.

Elliott, Russell R. *History of Nevada.* Lincoln: University of Nebraska Press, 1973.

———. *Nevada's Twentieth-Century Mining Boom: Tonopah, Goldfield, Ely.* Reno: University of Nevada Press, 1966.

Fleischmann Foundation. *Max C. Fleischmann Foundation: Twenty-Eight Years. A Narrative Report of the Foundation's Activities.* 1980.

Ford, Jean. *A Nevada Woman Shows the Way.* From oral interviews conducted and edited by Victoria Ford. Reno: University of Nevada Oral History Program, 1998.

Garrison, Dee. *Apostles of Culture: The Public Librarian and American Society, 1876–1920.* New York: Free Press, 1979.

Hildenbrand, Suzanne, ed. *Reclaiming the American Library Past: Writing the Women In.* Norwood, N.J.: Albex Publishing Co., 1996.

Howard, Anne Bail. *The Long Campaign: A Biography of Anne Martin.* Reno: University of Nevada Press, 1985.

Hulse, James W. *The Silver State: Nevada's History Reinterpreted.* 2d ed. Reno: University of Nevada Press, 1998.

——. *The University of Nevada: A Centennial History.* Reno: University of Nevada Press, 1974.

James, Ronald M. *Temples of Justice: County Courthouses of Nevada.* Foreword by Cliff Young. Reno: University of Nevada Press, 1994.

Jones, Theodore. *Carnegie Libraries across America: A Public Legacy.* New York: John Wiley & Sons, 1997.

Leigh, Robert D. *The Public Library in the United States.* New York: Columbia University Press, 1950.

McBride, Dennis. *In the Beginning . . . : A History of Boulder City, Nevada.* 2d ed., rev. and enl. Boulder City: Hoover Dam Museum, 1992.

McCracken, Robert D. *A History of Tonopah, Nevada.* Tonopah: Nye County Press, 1992.

Martin, Lowell A. *Enrichment: A History of the Public Library in the United States in the Twentieth Century.* Lanham, Md.: Scarecrow Press, 1998.

Moehring, Eugene P. *Resort City in the Sunbelt: Las Vegas, 1930–1970.* Reno: University of Nevada Press, 1989.

Nevada Library Association. *Intellectual Freedom Handbook. 1994.* Carson City: Nevada Library Association, 1994.

Maule, Wynne M. *Minden, Nevada: The Story of a Unique Town, 1906–1992.* Minden: Wynne M. Maule, 1993.

Passet, Joanne E. *Cultural Crusaders: Women Librarians in the Amercan West, 1900–1917.* Albuquerque: University of New Mexico Press, 1994.

Schenk, Gretchen Knief. *Public Library Service in Nevada* (1958). In *Appendix to the Journal of the Senate and Assembly.* 1959.

Van Slyk, Abigail A. *Free to All: Carnegie Libraries and American Culture, 1890–1920.* Chicago: University of Chicago Press, 1995.

Watson, Anita Ernst. *Into Their Own: Nevada Women Emerging into Public Life.* Reno: Nevada Humanities Committee, 2000.

Articles

Billington, James H. "American Public Libraries in the Information Age: Constant Purpose in Changing Times." *Libraries and Culture* 33, no. 1 (winter 1988).

Castagna, Edward. "Censorship, Intellectual Freedom, and Libraries." In *Advances in Librarianship.* Vol. 2. New York: Academic Press, 1971.

Coakley, Dee. "Our Libraries: How They Began." *Las Vegas Sun Magazine,* March 27, 1983, 8–9, April 3, 1983, 8–9.

"First Report: Nevada Libraries—1966." *Nevada Council on Libraries* (January 1967): 9.

InfoConnection: Nevada State Library and Archives 2, no. 4 (October–December 1992): 7.

Mathews, Barbara, and Dora Witt. "Churchill County Library: A Place for the Reader." *Churchill County: In Focus.* Annual journal of the Churchill County Museum Association. Fallon: 1987–88.

Polson, Billie Mae. "History of the Nevada Library Association." Adapted in 1980 from *Encylopedia of Library and Information Science* (New York: Marcel Dekker, 1976), 19:307–16. Typescript available in Nevada Library Assocation files, Special Collections Department, Getchell Library, University of Nevada, Reno.

Rhyno, Dick. "Brief History of the Washoe County Library System." *High Roller* 20, no. 2 (1983): 25.

Shipler, Guy. "Nevada's Libraries Malnourished." *Nevada State Record* (April 9, 1985).

Taylor, Sharon Lee. "Hidden Treasures of Churchill County." Newsprint. April 20, 1985. Churchill County Library.

Newspapers

Elko Daily Free Press. April 7, 1984.

Goldfield Chronicle. February 25, 1909.

Gold Hill News. November 11, 1965.

Lahontan Valley News & Fallon Eagle Standard. March 2, 1992.

Las Vegas Review Journal. September 30, 1968.

Las Vegas Sun. January 17, 1971, January 2, 1980.

Las Vegas Sun Magazine. March 22, April 3, 1983.

Lincoln County Record (Panaca). December 20, 1990.

Lovelock Review Miner. June 20, 1930.

Mineral County Independent. April 8, 1981.

Nevada Appeal. January 15, 1997.

Nevada State Journal. January 23, 1901, October 17, 1948.

Reno Evening Gazette. December 7, 1887, January 22, 1966.

Reno Gazette-Journal. July 15, 1979, March 31, 1986.

Sagebrush (University of Nevada, Reno). November 17, 1939.

Silver State (Winnemucca). February 8, 1923.

Sparks Tribune. April 9, 1980.

Territorial Enterprise (Virginia City). March 31, 1867, June 1, 1870.

White Pine News. March 12, July 16, 1916, April 1, 1917.

State of Nevada and County Publications

Las Vegas–Clark County. Library District. *The Decade of Expansion: 1979–1989 & 1990 Yearbook.* 1990.

Nevada. *Annual Reports of the Territorial Auditor, Treasurer, Superintendent of Public Instruction, and Adjutant General.* Carson City: Territorial Printer, 1864.

———. Biennial Reports of the State Library Commission.

———. *Biennial Report of the Superintendent of Public Instruction, 1903–1904.* Carson City: State Printing Office, 1905.

———. *Dateline.* Newsletter of the Nevada State Library.

———. Department of Museums, Library, and Arts. *Nevada Library Directory and Statistics: 2001.* Carson City, 2001.

———. *Laws of the Territory of Nevada.* 1861. Chapter 89, p. 295.

———. Legislative Counsel Bureau. *Legislation Toward Effective Library and Related Services for the People of Nevada.* Bulletin no. 25. December 1954.

———. Legislative Counsel Bureau. *The University of Nevada: An Appraisal.* Report of the University Survey. Bulletin no. 28. December 1956.

———. Nevada Historical Society. "Secretary's Report." In *First Biennial Report of the Nevada Historical Society 1907–1908.* Carson City: State Printing Office, 1909.

———. *Nevada State Library—Report.* July 1964–June 1966.

———. Nevada State Library. "Biennial Report of the Secretary of State and Ex Officio State Librarian." In *Appendix to the Journal of the Senate and Assembly, 1913–1914.* 1915.

———. Nevada State Library. "Biennial Report of the State Librarian." In *Appendix to the Journal of the Senate and Assembly.* 1946.

———. Nevada State Library. "Report of Librarian." In *Appendix to the Journal of the Senate and Assembly.* 1893.

———. Nevada State Library. "Report of State Librarian." In "Report of the Secretary of State," *Appendix to the Journal of the Senate and Assembly.* 1913.

———. Nevada State Library. "Report of the State Librarian." In "Biennial Report of the Secretary of State," *Appendix to the Journal of the Senate and Assembly.* 1899.

———. Nevada State Library. "Report of the State Librarian for the Years 1887–1888." In *Appendix to the Journal of the Senate and Assembly.* 1889.

———. Nevada State Library and Archives. *Libraries: Key to Democracy.* Governor's Conference on the Future of Libraries. Discussion Papers. Edited by Bonnie Buckley. February 1990.

———. *Statutes of the State of Nevada.* 1865–2001.

———. University of Nevada. Board of Regents. Reports.

———. *University of Nevada Report to the Commission of the Northwest Association of Secondary and Higher Schools.* 1958. Typescript in University of Nevada, Reno, Archives.

———. University of Nevada, Las Vegas. *Undergraduate Catalog, 1998–2000.*

———. University of Nevada, Reno. *General Catalog, 1999–2000.*

———. University of Nevada, Reno. *Institutional Self-Study Report for the Commission on Colleges, Northwest Association of Schools and Colleges.* Vol. 2. October 1988.

Washoe County. *Final Report of the Citizens' Blue Ribbon Advisory Committee on the Future of Washoe County Library.* February 1987.

U.S. Government Publications

U.S. *Congressional Record.* 84th Cong., 2d sess., 1956. Vol. 102, pt. 6.

———. Department of Education. Office of Educational Research and Improvement. *Public Libraries in the U.S.: 1990.* By E. D. Tabs. National Center for Education Statistics. June 1992.

————. Department of Education. *Public Libraries in the United States: FY 1995*. By E. D. Tabs. National Center for Education Statistics. August 1998.

————. Department of the Interior. *Public Libraries.* Washington, D.C.: Government Printing Office, 1875.

————. Department of the Interior, Bureau of Education. *Public Libraries in the United States of America . . . Special Report.* Pt. 1 (1876).

————. *Report of the Secretary of the Interior.* Washington, D.C.: Government Printing Office, 1894.

UNPUBLISHED SOURCES

Breen, Martha. "A Brief History of the Miners' Union Library of Virginia City, Nevada." Special Collections Department. Getchell Library, University of Nevada, Reno.

Brown, Alice. "Memorable Moments: The first 25 Years of the Library at the University of Nevada at Las Vegas." Typescript. Special Collections. University of Nevada, Las Vegas, Library.

Greenhaw, Charles. "People's Colleges." Manuscript of interviews with founders of community colleges in Nevada. Great Basin College, Elko, Nevada.

Hill, James J. "A Short History of the University of Nevada Libraries." Special Collections Department. Getchell Library, University of Nevada, Reno.

Johnson, Clare L. "History of the University of Nevada Library: 1876–1927." Special Collections Department. Getchell Library, University of Nevada, Reno.

Marden, J. P. "Early Winnemucca Libraries." Typescript. Humboldt County Library, Winnemucca, Nevada.

Nevada Library Association. Files. Special Collections Department. Getchell Library, University of Nevada, Reno.

————. Newsletters (*Nevada Librarian, High Roller*). Special Collections Department. Getchell Library, University of Nevada, Reno.

Nevada State Library. Files, history of Nevada libraries.

Newman, Linda P. "Early Public Libraries of Nevada." Typescript. May

1969. Special Collections Department. Getchell Library, University of Nevada, Reno.

Stephens, John Thompson. "Political Control over Special Districts in Local Government: A Case Study of the Las Vegas–Clark County Library District." Master's thesis, UNLV, May 1996.

Index

conference on library and information needs, 35; population of, 79, 82, 118; and regional library services, 27; and state bond money, 36; suburbs of, 29; wartime boom of, 81–82

Las Vegas Artists' League, 85

Las Vegas–Clark County Library District (LVCCLD), 87–90. *See also* Clark County Library District; Las Vegas public library

Las Vegas public library: and budget, 81, 82; buildings of, 86; collection of, 20; founding of, 56, 80; and library board, 87; and North Las Vegas public library, 92; and University of Nevada, Las Vegas library, 109. *See also* Clark County Library District

Laughlin public library, 88

laws and legislation: and bookmobile services, 21; and censorship, 41; and county commissioners, 65; and "fair share" distribution of state-support funds, 50; and Great Basin College, 115; and intercounty library districts, 63; and library construction, 17, 31–32, 36, 52; and library petitions, 8, 25, 32, 44, 83–84; and Nevada Library Association, 22, 31–33, 36, 40; and Nevada State Library and Archives, 13–14, 17, 18, 23, 38; and Newlands Reclamation Project, 1–2; and public library

policy, 9; and restructuring of 1965, 31–33; and rural libraries, 22–23; and school district library funds, 17; and Sparks library movement, 52; and state bond money, 36–37, 48; and support funding for books, library materials, and databases, 39; and surveys of Nevada libraries, 24–27; and tax-supported libraries, 3, 8, 9, 25, 26, 27, 36, 44; and University of Nevada, Las Vegas library, 111; and University of Nevada, Reno library, 96, 97, 101, 102, 103, 106; and Washoe County library board, 46

lawyers, 1

Layman, Joseph D., 97, 99

Lee, Clark "Danny," 87, 89

Legislative Counsel Bureau, 24–25

Leigh, Robert D., 23–24, 82

librarians: and censorship, 41; certification of, 27, 31; and Clark County Library District, 87; and First Aamendment, 23; and Nevada Library Association, 21–22, 56; Prentiss's attempts at organizing, 56; role of, 80; salaries of, 8; training for, 3, 22, 23, 24, 26–27, 31, 32, 88, 96

Library Bill of Rights (1939), 23

library boards: and Clark County Library District, 87, 89; commitment of, 5; and legislation, 8, 27, 44, 65; and Nevada Li-

brary Association, 22, 40; of
Nevada State Library and Archives, 13–14, 26; and Reno
public library, 44; and Schenk's
survey, 26; and Washoe County
Public Library System, 50, 51,
52–53
library construction: and Boulder
City Library, 91; and Carnegie,
10–11; and Carson City Library, 72; and Clark County
Library District, 85, 87–88; and
county government, 62, 67, 68,
69, 86; and Douglas County
public library, 73–74; and Elko
public library, 63; and Fallon
public library, 67; and federal
government, 30, 66, 67, 68–69,
71–72, 75, 84, 86; and Fleischmann Foundation, 30, 33–34,
36; and Kerschner's administration, 39; and legislation, 17, 31–
32, 36, 52; and local governments, 32, 33, 82, 86, 92; and
Lovelock public library, 66–67;
and Pahrump public library, 59;
and state government, 39, 58,
91; and Tonopah public library,
58; and University of Nevada,
Reno library, 98, 101, 103
Library of Congress, 90
library petitions: and county government, 8, 9, 44, 61; and legislation, 8, 25, 32, 44, 83–84; and
tax-supported libraries, 8, 9, 25,
44, 84, 90–91, 109

library services: children's services,
40, 60, 63, 66, 90; and Fleischmann Foundation, 34; and
governor's conference on library and information needs,
35; and Hunsberger, 89; Nevada
Council on Libraries' study of,
29–30; and Public Library Inquiry, 82; regional library services, 27, 33, 64; in rural counties, 4, 22, 29, 30, 61; Schenk's
survey of, 25–27; and Washoe
County Public Library System,
46–47, 49. *See also* bookmobile
services
Library Services Act (LSA), 27, 30,
65
Library Services and Construction
Act (LSCA), 30, 62, 63
library trustees. *See* library boards
Lied Children's Discovery Museum, 90
Lied Foundation, 111
lieutenant governor, and Nevada
State Library and Archives, 14,
15
Lincoln County, 57, 69–71, 88
Lion's Club (Lovelock), 66
literary societies, 8, 14, 44, 67
local governments: and
Fleischmann Foundation, 33;
and library construction, 32, 33,
82, 86, 92; and library districts,
92; and library funding, 27, 30,
80, 91; and library petitions, 79;
and rural libraries, 56–57, 59,

regional library services, 27, 33, 64
Reno, Nev.: economy of, 43, 44–
45; libraries of, 43–51; and Nevada Library Association, 21,
22; population of, 9, 10, 91; and
regional library services, 27
Reno public library: buildings of,
45, 46, 51–52; and Carnegie, 10,
11, 16–17, 45, 56; collection of,
20, 45–46, 47, 48; as first Nevada library, 3, 4, 16–17, 43, 56;
and library petition, 83, 84; and
Norcross, 9, 10, 22, 32, 43, 44,
55, 56, 122 n. 13; services of,
46–47; as tax-supported library,
44; usage of, 46. *See also* Washoe
County Public Library System
Reno school district, 10, 46
Ring, Orvis, 17
Rio Tinto, Nev., 21
Robert Zimmer Hawkins Foundation, 106
Rocha, Guy Louis, 41–42
Rose, Mary G., 65
Round Mountain public library, 59
rural counties: and library consolidation, 58; library services in, 4,
22, 29, 30, 61; male/female
population of, 56; and state
bond money, 36; and women's
activism, 84
rural libraries: and Cooperative
Libraries Automated Network,
77; and Fleischmann, 20; and
Fleischmann Foundation, 33;
and Kerschner, 39; and legisla-

tion, 22–23; and Library Services Act, 27; and state government, 60
Ruth, Nev., 61

Sandy Valley public library, 88
Sawyer, Grant, 83, 102
Schenk, Gretchen Knief, 25, 26,
33, 47, 82
school-district library funds, 17
school libraries, 17, 23, 24, 51, 52
Schubert, Joseph F., 27, 30–31, 66
scientific societies, 14
Scrugham, James G., 65
Searchlight public library, 88
secretary of state: clerk of, as li-
brarian, 8; as ex officio state li-
brarian, 13, 15, 17, 18; and Ne-
vada State Library and Archives
budget, 14
Shipler, Guy, 37
Shirkey, Dorothy, 59
Sierra Nevada College, 77
Sierra View branch library, 49–50
Silver Circle, 31
Silver Peak public library, 75
Silver Springs branch library, 69
Six Companies, 90
Sloan, Mrs. Charles, 80
Smith, Hardin E., 85
Smith Valley branch library, 69
Smoky Valley Library District, 59
Social Science Research Council,
23, 82
social service organizations, 51, 56
Southern Pacific Railroad, 51